Investigating the INFLUENCE OF STANDARDS

A Framework for Research in Mathematics, Science, and Technology Education

Committee on Understanding the Influence of Standards in K-12 Science, Mathematics, and Technology Education

Iris R. Weiss, Michael S. Knapp, Karen S. Hollweg, and Gail Burrill, editors

Center for Education
Division of Behavioral and Social Sciences and Education
National Research Council

NATIONAL ACADEMY PRESS
Washington, DC

NATIONAL ACADEMY PRESS • 2101 Constitution Avenue, NW • Washington, DC 20418

NOTICE: The project that is the subject of this report was approved by the Governing Board of the National Research Council, whose members are drawn from the councils of the National Academy of Sciences, the National Academy of Engineering, and the Institute of Medicine. The members of the committee responsible for the report were chosen for their special competences and with regard for appropriate balance.

This study was supported by Contract/Grant No. ESI-9618770 between the National Academy of Sciences and the National Science Foundation. Any opinions, findings, conclusions, or recommendations expressed in this publication are those of the author(s) and do not necessarily reflect the views of the organizations or agencies that provided support for the project.

Library of Congress Cataloging-in-Publication Data

Investigating the influence of standards : a framework for research in mathematics, science, and technology education / Iris R. Weiss ... [et al.].

p. cm.

Includes bibliographical references and index.

ISBN 0-309-07276-X (pbk.)

1. Mathematics—Study and teaching—Standards—United States—Evaluation. 2. Science—Study and teaching—Standards—United States—Evaluation. 3. Technical education—Standards—United States—Evaluation. I. Weiss, Iris R.

QA13 .I55 2001

507.1′073—dc21

2001006094

Additional copies of this report are available from National Academy Press, 2101 Constitution Avenue, NW, Lockbox 285, Washington, DC 20055; (800) 624-6242 or (202) 334-3313 (in the Washington metropolitan area); Internet, http://www.nap.edu

Printed in the United States of America

Suggested citation: National Research Council. (2002). *Investigating the influence of standards: A framework for research in mathematics, science, and technology education.* I.R. Weiss, M.S. Knapp, K.S. Hollweg, and G. Burrill (Eds.), Committee on Understanding the Influence of Standards in K-12 Science, Mathematics, and Technology Education, Center for Education, Division of Behavioral and Social Sciences and Education. Washington, DC: National Academy Press.

THE NATIONAL ACADEMIES

National Academy of Sciences
National Academy of Engineering
Institute of Medicine
National Research Council

The **National Academy of Sciences** is a private, nonprofit, self-perpetuating society of distinguished scholars engaged in scientific and engineering research, dedicated to the furtherance of science and technology and to their use for the general welfare. Upon the authority of the charter granted to it by the Congress in 1863, the Academy has a mandate that requires it to advise the federal government on scientific and technical matters. Dr. Bruce M. Alberts is president of the National Academy of Sciences.

The **National Academy of Engineering** was established in 1964, under the charter of the National Academy of Sciences, as a parallel organization of outstanding engineers. It is autonomous in its administration and in the selection of its members, sharing with the National Academy of Sciences the responsibility for advising the federal government. The National Academy of Engineering also sponsors engineering programs aimed at meeting national needs, encourages education and research, and recognizes the superior achievements of engineers. Dr. Wm. A. Wulf is president of the National Academy of Engineering.

The **Institute of Medicine** was established in 1970 by the National Academy of Sciences to secure the services of eminent members of appropriate professions in the examination of policy matters pertaining to the health of the public. The Institute acts under the responsibility given to the National Academy of Sciences by its congressional charter to be an adviser to the federal government and, upon its own initiative, to identify issues of medical care, research, and education. Dr. Kenneth I. Shine is president of the Institute of Medicine.

The **National Research Council** was organized by the National Academy of Sciences in 1916 to associate the broad community of science and technology with the Academy's purposes of furthering knowledge and advising the federal government. Functioning in accordance with general policies determined by the Academy, the Council has become the principal operating agency of both the National Academy of Sciences and the National Academy of Engineering in providing services to the government, the public, and the scientific and engineering communities. The Council is administered jointly by both Academies and the Institute of Medicine. Dr. Bruce M. Alberts and Dr. Wm. A. Wulf are chairman and vice chairman, respectively, of the National Research Council.

COMMITTEE ON UNDERSTANDING THE INFLUENCE OF STANDARDS IN K-12 SCIENCE, MATHEMATICS, AND TECHNOLOGY EDUCATION

Iris R. Weiss (Chair), Horizon Research, Inc.
William Browder, Princeton University
Maria Alicia Lopez Freeman, California Science Project, University of California, Los Angeles
Michael Fullan, Ontario Institute for Studies in Education, University of Toronto
Margaret Goertz, Consortium for Policy Research in Education, University of Pennsylvania
Michael S. Knapp, Center for the Study of Teaching and Policy, University of Washington
Paul LeMahieu, Hawaii Department of Education
Mari Muri, Connecticut Department of Education
Patrick M. Shields, SRI International
Judith Sowder, Department of Mathematical and Computer Science, San Diego State University
Elizabeth K. Stage, Office of the President, University of California
Kendall Starkweather, International Technology Education Association
P. Uri Treisman, The Charles A. Dana Center for Mathematics and Science Education, University of Texas at Austin
Marc Tucker, The National Center on Education and the Economy

Staff, Center for Education

Karen S. Hollweg, Project Director
Gail Burrill, Senior Program Officer
Tina Winters, Senior Project Assistant*
Viola Horek, Administrative Associate**
Henry Heikkinen, Consultant Writer/Editor

*Through March 2001
**Since March 2001

COMMITTEE ON SCIENCE EDUCATION K-12

J. Myron Atkin (Chair), School of Education, Stanford University
Carol Brewer, Division of Biological Sciences, University of Montana
Caryl Edward Buchwald,* Carleton College
George Bugliarello,** Polytechnic University
Elizabeth A. Carvellas,* Chittenden Central School District, Vermont
Christine Chopyak-Minor,**** Keystone Science School, Colorado
Beatrice Chu Clewell,*** Urban Institute
Peter B. Dow,**** First Hand Learning, Inc.
William E. Dugger, Jr.,* International Technology Education Association
Hubert Dyasi, City College (City University of New York)
Wade Ellis, Jr.,**** West Valley College
Maria Alicia Lopez Freeman, California Science Project
Norman Hackerman,* The Robert A. Welch Foundation
Patty Harmon, San Francisco Unified School District
Robert M. Hazen,**** Carnegie Institute of Washington
Leroy Hood,** Institute for Systems Biology
Anne Jolly, SERVE
Jane Butler Kahle,**** Miami University, Ohio
Michael G. Lang,**** Maricopa Community College
Ron Latanision, Massachusetts Institute of Technology
William Linder-Scholer, SciMathMN
Jim Minstrell, Talaria Inc.
John A. Moore,** University of California, Riverside
Darlene Norfleet,** Flynn Park Elementary School, Missouri
Carolyn L. Ray,* Urban Systemic Initiative, Euclid, Ohio
Cary I. Sneider, Boston Museum of Science
William E. Spooner,*** CBSG
Judith Sydner-Gordon,**** Los Angeles County Office of Education
Jerry Valadez, Fresno Unified School District
Rachel Wood,* Delaware State Department of Education
Robert Yinger, School of Education, Baylor University

---

*Term ended January 2001
**Term ended January 2000
***Term ended July 1999
****Term ended January 1999

MATHEMATICAL SCIENCES EDUCATION BOARD

ACKNOWLEDGMENTS

This report could not have happened without support from a number of people, and I am grateful for their contributions. On behalf of the Committee on Understanding the Influence of Standards in Science, Mathematics, and Technology Education, I want first of all to acknowledge our sponsor, the National Science Foundation, and in particular Janice Earle and Jane Butler Kahle for making this project possible.

A number of former staff members from the Center for Science, Mathematics, and Engineering Education (the precursor to the current Center for Education) were instrumental in getting this project off the ground. Susan Loucks-Horsley was the initial project director and saw the Committee through the first year of its work. The former executive and associate executive directors, Rodger Bybee and Joan Ferrini-Mundy, conceptualized the project and provided ongoing support. Their presentations on the nationally developed science and mathematics standards were invaluable to the Committee. Harold Pratt, former director of the Center's Division on K-12 Policy and Practice, gave ongoing advice throughout the first year of the project. Kristance Coates, the former senior project assistant, provided essential support during the early months of the Committee's work. We are also grateful to Suzanne Woolsey, the Center's acting director in fall 1999, for her vigilance in seeing that this project received the support it needed during the Center's transition.

The Committee was aided greatly by individuals who participated in our meetings and helped us understand the complex issues involved in examining how nationally developed mathematics, science, and technology standards have influenced K-12 education in the United States. The participants in the May 2000 workshop, listed in Appendix A, also very generously gave two days of their time to discuss the Committee's work and provided critical input for the final stages of the Committee's work following the workshop.

Many others have supported this project. The Mathematical Sciences Education Board and the Committee on Science Education K-12 provided oversight and advice to the Committee throughout the project. Several individuals provided advice along the way, including Richard Askey, Audrey Champagne, James J. Gallagher, Daniel Heck, Thomas Romberg, and Mark St. John. Joan Ferrini-Mundy and Harold Pratt, who were instrumental in the early stages of the project, rejoined our efforts in the final stages of the project, providing in-depth comments and advice on drafts of the report. Tina Winters and Viola Horek provided valuable support, coordinated many aspects of the project, and were important in seeing that the project moved forward.

The Committee was resolute in working through the many difficult issues that arose until we achieved consensus on the document. Special thanks are due to Mike Knapp, whose substantial written contributions throughout the process led us to include him as an editor, and to a subset of the Committee that participated in numerous conference calls and attended informal meetings, e.g., at the American Educational Research Association Annual Meeting, as we continued to hammer out the details: Peg Goertz, Mike Knapp, Maria Alicia Lopez Freeman, Patrick Shields, Judy Sowder, and Elizabeth Stage. And it is certainly no exaggeration to say that without the ceaseless support from National Research Council (NRC) staff members Karen Hollweg and Gail Burrill, this document would never have seen the light of day.

This report has been reviewed in draft form by individuals chosen for their diverse perspectives and technical expertise, in accordance with procedures approved by the NRC Report Review Committee. The purpose of this independent review is to provide candid and critical comments that will assist the institution in making its published report as sound as possible and to ensure that the report meets institutional standards for objectivity, evidence, and responsiveness to the study charge. The review comments and draft manuscript remain confidential to protect the integrity of the deliberative process. We wish to thank the following individuals for their review of this report:

Henry L. Alder, University of California, Davis
Lynn Cornett, Southern Regional Education Board, Atlanta, GA
Karen Economopolous, TERC, Cambridge, MA
Manuel Gomez, University of Puerto Rico
Daniel Koretz, RAND, Arlington, VA
Ronald M. Latanision, Massachusetts Institute of Technology
Bill Linder-Scholer, SciMathMN, Roseville, MN
Roland J. Otto, E.O. Lawrence Berkeley National Laboratory, Berkeley, CA
Richard Satchwell, Illinois State University
Scott Stowell, Spokane Public Schools, WA

Although the reviewers listed above have provided many constructive comments and suggestions, they were not asked to endorse the conclusions or recommendations nor did they see the final draft of the report before its release. The review of this report was overseen by Michael W. Kirst, Stanford University, and R. Stephen Berry, University of Chicago. Appointed by the National Research Council, they were responsible for making certain that an independent examination of this report was carried out in accordance with institutional procedures and that all review comments were carefully considered. Responsibility for the final content of this report rests entirely with the authoring committee and the institution.

Iris R. Weiss, Chair
Committee on Understanding the Influence of Standards in Science, Mathematics, and Technology Education

PREFACE

Standards have served as a basis of educational reform across the nation as educators and policy makers respond to the call for a clear definition of desired outcomes of schooling and a way to measure student success in terms of these outcomes. Public policies at the federal, state, and local levels have focused on standards as a way to raise achievement levels for all students. At the national level, content standards have been developed in nearly every academic discipline.

As the standards movement has gained momentum, there has been increasing interest among educators and the public concerning the impact of standards on what happens in classrooms. In response to this interest, and as part of its mission of working for improved mathematics and science teaching and learning across the nation, the National Research Council's Center for Science, Mathematics, and Engineering Education (which became the Center for Education in 2000)—with funding from the National Science Foundation—undertook the task of designing a framework that would aid in the design, conduct, and interpretation of research regarding the influence on student learning of the standards created at the national level in mathematics, science, and technology. In 1999, the Committee on Understanding the Influence of Standards in K-12 Science, Mathematics, and Technology Education began its work. The charge of the Committee was to "develop a framework that can be used to understand the influence of science, mathematics, and technology education standards on programs, policies, and practices." This Framework was to provide guidance for the design, conduct, and interpretation of research regarding the influences of nationally developed standards on student learning in mathematics, science, and technology education. Hence, the Committee's primary concern has been to develop a structure and process for understanding the influence of these educational standards on practices, programs, and policies in K-12 education. The Committee was responsible to two standing boards in the Center, the Committee on K-12 Science Education (COSE K-12) and the Mathematical Sciences Education Board (MSEB), and the Committee's work reflects the oversight of these two boards.

An overarching problem faced by the Committee was how to structure thinking about the impact of standards in a way that would consider the complex system in which the standards operate—a system that consists of several layers of policy makers, various educators involved in multiple ways, and an array of players with different responsibilities for what takes place in classrooms. It was clear from the beginning that we were not to answer the question of what influence the standards have had on educational reform. It was a constant struggle, however, to keep the focus on a framework and not an analysis of where and how the standards had taken root in education systems and whether they were affecting student learning.

As the Committee worked, we came to a common understanding of some of the issues in the daunting task of laying out a way to think about the influence of the nationally developed standards on what happens within this complex system and eventually on what happens to student learning. We agreed, for example, to focus our thinking on separate but interacting channels within the education system—curriculum, teacher development, and assessment and accountability—and to consider how reform ideas might traverse these channels to reach the classroom. At the same time, we recognized that contextual forces outside the education system, in the public and political world, directly and indirectly affect what happens in the classroom, and we wanted to be sure the Framework considered those as well. We agreed to concentrate on the standards created by the National Council of Teachers of Mathematics, the National Research Council, and the International Technology Education Association that focus on teaching and learning in mathematics, science, and technology. We also agreed that the focus of our work was not on the quality of the standards documents themselves but rather on their influence. We did not analyze the nationally developed documents nor make judgments about their focus and content, but concentrated on developing ways to think about whether and how these standards were being used in the system and with what results.

As our work progressed, we came to see even more clearly the importance of having the document be neutral, neither advocating nor denigrating the standards and their impact. Our work was to lay out questions that should be answered in order to come to understand the influence of standards, regardless of whether or not the answers supported the thinking in the national documents. The Framework presented in this document is the result of our discussions.

We eventually came to agree that the Framework would describe the system in which the standards operate, then suggest places where the effect of the standards might be observed in this system, which became the organizing structure of the document. We have drawn on a broad body of research related to various aspects of the task, and have also relied heavily on the practical experience of the Committee members and outside experts in designing the Framework. The Committee produced a background paper for its work, and in spring 2000, convened a group of educators and researchers in a workshop to discuss and critique the paper. The Committee used the insights and input from workshop participants to help define the Framework and to stimulate ideas regarding its future uses.

Investigating the Influence of Standards is aimed at researchers and those who use research in their work, including federal, state, and local policy makers. It is intended to provide a lens for considering the national standards and the role such standards play in improving mathematics, science, and technology education. This book is not intended to be a simple template prescribing a solution but rather lays out the major issues involved in considering the effects of standards in improving student learning, offering questions that should be asked when considering research about the standards. The document can be used to understand particular studies, to identify what the studies do and do not address, and to help consumers interpret their claims. The document is also designed to spur additional research in areas where answers to the questions are not well-formed. While the focus of this document is the nationally developed standards in mathematics, science, and technology, we believe the Framework is general enough to serve as a guide for those at state and district levels and in other disciplines to analyze the impact of their own standards.

Iris R. Weiss, Chair
Committee on Understanding the Influence of Standards in Science, Mathematics, and Technology Education

CONTENTS

FIGURES, BOXES, AND TABLE

Figures

Boxes

Table

EXECUTIVE SUMMARY

Education in the United States operates within a complex system. It is difficult to focus on any particular component without considering how it is influenced by and, in turn, influences other parts of the education system. Standards created at the national level began working their way into this multifaceted system starting in the late 1980s. Over time, the standards movement grew to include mathematics, science, and technology standards on content, teaching, assessment, and professional development, as well as standards specifying the support needed from the education system and public. Those standards have been defined in documents published by the National Council of Teachers of Mathematics (NCTM), the National Research Council (NRC), and the International Technology Education Association (ITEA). Now, more than a decade into the standards movement, the key questions concern the impact of those standards.

The charge to the Committee that produced this document was to "develop a framework that can be used to understand the influence of science, mathematics, and technology education standards on programs, policies, and practices." The Committee acknowledged early in its work that a body of research related to education standards is emerging—work that addresses questions of impact on student learning and other aspects of the education system. However, no comprehensive map or conceptual overview has been available to guide the efforts of producers, interpreters, and consumers of that standards-focused research. The Framework developed in this document is intended to address that need—to provide guidance for the design, conduct, and interpretation of research focused on influences of nationally developed standards on student learning in mathematics, science, and technology.

INTRODUCTION

Perspectives on Standards

To many educators, a "standard" is a statement describing what a person should know or be able to do. That use of "standard" is often called a "content standard." For many members of the general public and for the education policy community, "standards" focus on outcomes and imply "a mechanism by which to hold schools accountable for what students learn" (Raizen, 1998). In such cases, specific levels of performance relative to standards are defined, and assessments are designed to measure student progress toward attaining those standards.

NCTM, NRC, and ITEA "standards" use the word in a broader sense, offering a vision for what is needed to enable *all* students to become literate in mathematics, science, and technology. Teaching and learning promoted by the mathematics, science, and technology standards represent a departure from common patterns of practice. All three sets of standards affirm the importance of increased expectations, opportunities, and achievement of all students, including groups largely bypassed historically, such as girls and ethnic and language minorities. The standards call on teachers to recognize the rich diversity students bring to classrooms and to provide opportunities for all students to learn.

The standards emphasize understanding of basic concepts and "big ideas" in each subject area, acquisition of useful skills, engagement in inquiry-based learning, and coherent articulation of learning opportunities across all grade levels. The standards also call for students to be able to use their knowledge, skills, and understanding to make decisions and participate productively in society, as well as to solve problems and communicate their thinking and reasoning to others. However, the nationally developed standards deliberately leave specific curricular decisions to state and local officials.

The NCTM, NRC, and ITEA standards call for changes not only in what students learn, but also in how that content is taught. According to the standards documents, teachers should have deep understanding of the science, mathematics, and technology content they teach; recognize and address common student preconceptions; design classroom experiences that actively engage students in building their understanding; emphasize the use and application of what is learned; and use assessment as an integral part of instruction.

The U.S. Education System

While standards provide a vision for teaching and learning, the vision cannot be realized unless the standards permeate the education system. The U.S. education system is large, diverse, and complex, with many layers of governance. States play major roles in funding and regulating education. At the same time, what happens in individual classrooms is affected by decisions made in other layers of this loosely coupled system.

Based on research, interactions with practitioners in the field, and personal experiences, the authoring Committee chose three main routes or "channels" to describe paths through which reform ideas might flow to various layers of the system and might eventually influence teaching and learning. As reforms (such as standards) enter the education system, they traverse one or more of these "channels," and thus may affect policies, programs, and practices within various jurisdictional layers. The three major channels of influence identified by the Committee are: Curriculum, Teacher Development, and Assessment and Accountability. In addition, standards may have an impact on education's social and political contexts, perhaps spurring those outside the education system to influence, both directly and indirectly, what happens in classrooms.

THE FRAMEWORK

Based on this view of the education system and its charge, the Committee identified two overarching questions: *How has the system responded to the introduction of nationally developed mathematics, science, and technology standards?* and *What are the consequences for student learning?* The Committee created a Framework to provide guidance in answering these questions. It consists of a conceptual map that identifies the channels through which nationally developed standards may influence teaching practice and subsequently student learning, and a set of guiding questions that can be applied to various policies, programs, and practices within the system and to outside influences that may affect the education system. As configured, the Framework provides conceptual guideposts for those attempting to trace the influence of nationally developed mathematics, science, and technology standards and to gauge the magnitude or direction of that influence on the education system, on teachers and teaching practice, and on student learning.

As is true for all models, the system represented in the Framework is greatly simplified. The argument implied by the Framework can be summarized through a group of interrelated propositions:

- Nationally developed standards in mathematics, science, and technology represent a set of fundamental changes in the way these subjects have traditionally been taught, placing new demands on teachers and students.
- The expected influence of nationally developed standards on teaching practice and student learning is likely to be (a) indirect, taking place through proximate effects on other parts of the education system; (b) entangled (and sometimes confused) with other

influential forces and conditions, such as broader state standards-based reforms; and (c) slowly realized and long term.

- Three core channels exist within the education system through which nationally developed standards can influence teaching and learning; these channels of influence are complex, interactive, and differ across subject-matter communities.
- Variability within the education system implies that students and teachers are likely to experience different influences, depending on locality, resources, participant background, and other factors.
- The task for research—and hence for this Framework—is to help identify and document significant standards-based effects, as well as overall trends and patterns among those effects.
- Nationally developed standards will eventually be judged effective if resources, requirements, and practices throughout the system align with the standards and if students in standards-based classrooms demonstrate high achievement in knowledge and skills deemed important.

The Framework offers four key questions to guide inquiry into the magnitude and direction of the influence of standards on various parts of the education system:

How are nationally developed standards being received and interpreted? The vision expressed in the standards for student learning, teaching practice, and system behavior is conveyed through broadly framed statements, and as a consequence may be interpreted differently by different people. In investigating the influence of standards, it is important to understand how these standards are viewed by particular stakeholders.

What actions have been taken? Standards can motivate changes in the system or they may simply be ignored. An important part of tracing the influence of standards is understanding what curriculum developers, teacher educators, assessment designers, and others have done in response to standards.

What has changed as a result? In investigating the influence of standards, it is important to determine what new policies, programs, or practices can be attributed to the influence of standards. In particular, it would be important to know the extent to which K-12 classroom instruction reflects the content and pedagogy emphasized in the national standards documents.

Who has been affected and how? Nationally developed mathematics, science, and technology standards explicitly call for reform in policies and practice leading to literacy for *all* students. Investigating the influence of nationally developed standards requires understanding for whom teaching and learning have changed and how their learning has been affected.

CHANNELS OF INFLUENCE

The channels set forth in the Framework, through which reform ideas may flow, have different properties and points of interface with classroom practice.

Curriculum

The influence of nationally developed standards on what students are to learn is filtered through the forces and conditions that define the curriculum and instructional materials in mathematics, science, and technology. What is actually taught in classrooms in the United States is shaped by decisions made at multiple levels—the federal government, states, districts, schools, and individual teachers. Exploring what is taught to whom and why involves addressing the implications of a myriad of policy decisions that affect curriculum and resources to support the curriculum; the development of instructional materials and programs; and the processes and criteria for selecting instructional materials that help determine what students will learn in a particular classroom.

Nationally developed standards can influence the formulation and enactment of curriculum by providing a comprehensive picture of what should be taught, stimulating the creation or adoption of curricular materials that embody the standards' vision, and giving direction to the various entities that contribute to the development and adoption of instructional materials. If standards are influencing the curriculum channel, state content standards would be increasingly aligned with the national content standards; standards-based K-12 programs would be coordinated systemwide; textbooks would reflect an understanding of the content in the standards; and teachers would have appropriate resources for teaching standards-based lessons.

Teacher Development

The teacher preparation and development components within the education system provide channels through which nationally developed standards might influence how teachers learn to teach initially and throughout their careers. The policies, practices, and programs at local, state, and federal levels determine investments made in teaching prospective teachers and in molding the ways they continue to develop their skills as classroom teachers. Teachers' subject matter and pedagogical knowledge are shaped by their initial exposure to mathematics, science, and technology content—and the ways those subjects are taught—prior to and during their formal teacher preparation program and by the requirements for certification and licensure. Teachers' continuing professional learning may be enhanced or constrained by the setting within which they work and by the opportunities available to them.

If nationally developed standards are influencing the preparation of new teachers, states would require and postsecondary institutions would create systems that enable prospective teachers to gain the knowledge and skills needed to help students meet standards-based learning goals. Policies and fiscal investments at local, state, and federal levels would focus on re-certification criteria and ongoing professional development opportunities that align with nationally developed standards in the three subject areas. States and localities would provide a rich "infrastructure" to support standards-based mathematics, science, and technology teaching.

Assessment and Accountability

As the standards movement has gained strength across the United States, assessment and accountability, which are two distinct but related concepts, have become linked as a way to realize the standards, and as such constitute a third channel through which reform might flow. Assessments of various kinds provide systematic means of informing students, teachers, parents, the public, and policy makers about student performance. Accountability mechanisms linked to some or all of these assessments provide incentives to change behavior, by using information from assessments to make consequential decisions about students, teachers, schools, or districts. Thus, consideration of assessment involves a careful study of how assessment interacts with accountability; how teachers conduct and use classroom assessment; how states and districts use assessment for accountability; and how assessment influences choices in postsecondary education.

Assessment practices are vital components of nationally developed standards, specifying expectations for student knowledge and performance. The development and use of assessments to support instruction, to drive educational improvement, and to support accountability are indicators of possible influences attributable to nationally developed standards. If nationally developed standards are influencing assessment policies and practices, assessments would be aligned with learning outcomes embodied in the standards. Accountability policies would support schools and teachers by providing professional development opportunities, instructional materials, and appropriate resources to enhance their efforts to raise performance levels of their students.

CONTEXTUAL FORCES AS A SOURCE OF INFLUENCE

Decision-making within the education system is, in large part, a political process, involving key players such as legislators, government officials, and citizen groups, in addition to educators. Educational concerns may motivate professional organizations, parents, and others to lobby for certain decisions or work toward particular goals. Education policy decisions may also be influenced by media that convey information and shape public perceptions. In addition to exerting influence through the political system, some businesses, education and professional organizations, and others may influence the education system directly, for example, by supporting ongoing teacher professional development efforts.

If the standards are influencing individuals and groups external to the education system as intended, decisions enacted by elected officials and policy makers would show support for standards-based reforms. Professional associations in the forefront of the development of national standards for mathematics, science, and technology would lead national and local efforts to implement the standards, as well as work with elected officials and leaders to build a consensus in support of institutionalizing standards-based reforms.

On the other hand, standards may generate resistance and opposition by individuals and groups outside the system. In that case, scientists, mathematicians, engineers, and technology design professionals who disagree with the standards' vision would work to affect decisions and actions within the education system. Opponents would encourage funding or programmatic decisions regarding curriculum, professional development, and accountability practices that inhibit implementation of the nationally developed standards.

USING THE FRAMEWORK

The Framework in this document provides a set of organizing categories, presumed relationships among them, and questions to prompt inquiry. The Framework lays out a complex domain of interacting forces and conditions that affect teaching and learning, any number of which can be touched by the influence of standards.

Thus no single study can investigate the entire domain—that is, all the ways that national standards are, or could be, part of the education reform story. Rather, various types of studies, each guided by its own appropriate methodologies, will be needed to establish the scale and scope of influences, identify routes by which standards actually exert influence, and ascertain the direction and educational consequences of those influences.

The Framework is offered as a tool for producers, consumers, and sponsors of research as they consider central questions about the influence of nationally developed standards on mathematics, science, and technology education. It can be used in: (1) situating existing studies within the educational terrain relevant to the standards; (2) providing a conceptual tool for analyzing claims and inferences made by these studies; and (3) generating questions and hypotheses to be explored by future studies through assembling knowledge gained from existing studies and identifying gaps in current research. The Framework should be regarded as an evolving conceptual picture, stimulating different forms of inquiry, and helping to guard against the superficiality that often permeates debate about high-visibility national policies.

Public conversations about the worth and impact of standards in mathematics, science, and technology—or about standards-based reforms in general—will continue. The Framework offered here is intended to help the education research community contribute to that debate with reasoned voices based on evidence and sound inference.

CHAPTER 1

INTRODUCTION

Education in the United States operates within a complex system. It is difficult to focus on any particular component without considering how it is influenced by and, in turn, influences other parts of the education system. For example, what students learn is clearly related to what they are taught; which in turn depends on the intended curriculum; how teachers elect to use that curriculum; the kinds of resources teachers have for their instructional work; what the community values regarding student learning; and how local, state, and national assessments influence instructional practice.

Standards created at the national level began working their way into this complex education system starting in the late 1980s (McLeod, Stake, Schappelle, Melissinos, and Gierl, 1996). Over time, the standards movement grew to include standards on content, teaching, assessment, and professional development, as well as standards specifying the support needed from the education system and public. Throughout the 1990s, professional organizations, educators, and national and state leaders continued to articulate the vision that the nation's schools can and should support excellence and, more particularly, that *all* students should attain high learning goals (U.S. Department of Education [USDoE], 1991; National Educational Goals Panel [NEGP], 1996; USDoE, 2000b). Now, more than a decade into the standards movement, the overarching question concerns the impact of those standards on student learning.

This document provides a framework for thinking about the possible effects of nationally developed standards in three subject areas—mathematics, science, and technology. Those standards have been defined in documents published by the National Council of Teachers of Mathematics (NCTM) in *Curriculum and Evaluation Standards for School Mathematics* (1989), *Professional Standards for Teaching Mathematics* (1991), *Assessment Standards for School Mathematics* (1995), and *Principles and Standards for School Mathematics* (2000); by the National Research Council (NRC) in *National Science Education Standards* (1996); and by the International Technology Education Association (ITEA) in *Standards for Technological Literacy: Content for the Study of Technology* (2000).

Given that array of nationally developed standards, two related questions arise: *How has the system responded to the introduction of nationally developed standards?* and *What are the consequences for student learning?* In other words, what inferences can be made about what is happening in the "black box" between the development of national standards and any impact on student learning (Figure 1-1)?

The charge to the Committee that produced this document was to "develop a framework that can be used to understand the influence of science, mathematics, and technology education standards on programs, policies, and practices." The Committee acknowledged early in its work that a body of research related to education standards is emerging—work that addresses questions of

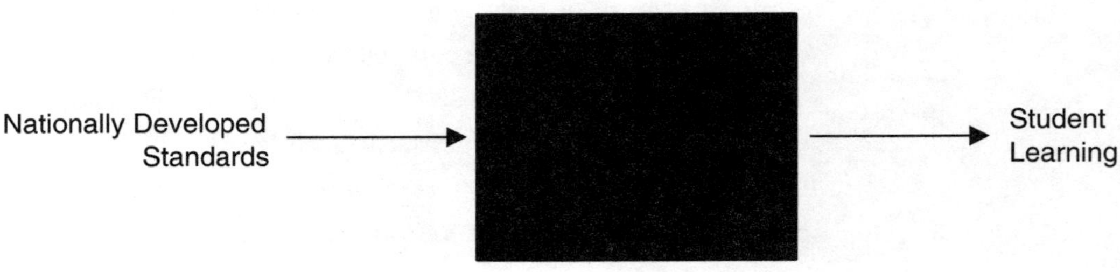

FIGURE 1-1 The Black Box

impact on student learning and other aspects of the education system. However, no comprehensive map or conceptual overview has been available to guide the efforts of producers, interpreters, and consumers of that standards-focused research. This Framework is intended to address that need—that is, to provide guidance for the design, conduct, and interpretation of research focused on influences of nationally developed standards on student learning in mathematics, science, and technology.

The Framework describes key leverage points, identifies questions that need answers, and considers how evidence can be assembled to address those questions. However, the Framework offers no judgments about the standards themselves or their effects on the education system. That is, it does not consider whether the quality of current mathematics, science, or technology education has improved or declined due to nationally developed standards. It neither advocates nor criticizes the standards, and does not attempt to synthesize or interpret existing research concerning influences of standards. Rather, this Framework offers guidance and perspective both to the research community and to those who use the results of such research—policy makers, educators, administrators, scholars, and members of the public. The Framework is dedicated to helping this audience to formulate, conduct, and interpret research about influences on student learning—either positive or negative—of nationally developed standards in mathematics, science, and technology education, whether the standards are generally accepted or considered controversial.

As indicated by their publication dates, the standards for the three subject areas were created at different times. It is thus reasonable to expect that each field will be at a different place regarding dissemination and implementation of its standards. Each field also occupies a different position within the context of education. Historically, mathematics has been regarded as a basic skill in the school curriculum. Its prominence from elementary school onward has thus been assured—even though for a considerable time, the notion of mathematical literacy for all did not extend beyond general numerical skills.

Science, although considered a "basic" in many states and districts, has not historically held a secure place in the K-12 curriculum. For example, instructional time allotted to science in elementary schools is generally much lower than time dedicated to reading or mathematics (Weiss, Matti, and Smith, 1994).

Technological literacy, as defined by the technology standards, is a relatively recent addition to the K-12 curriculum. Many educators seek clarity about the structure and form in which students should gain knowledge and skills associated with technology. For example, in many school systems debate continues about whether technology constitutes an area of discrete study or is a set of knowledge and skills that should be integrated into other school subjects.

Despite these variations, the Framework presented in this document is intended to allow both researchers and consumers of research to identify and analyze connections between standards and what students actually learn in these three subject areas. Although the Committee's charge was to focus on nationally developed standards for mathematics, science, and technology, the Committee believes that this Framework is more generally applicable and could be used to guide inquiries into the effects of state or local standards and also into the impact of standards in other areas of the school curriculum.

Investigating the Influence of Standards is divided into eight chapters. The document first describes the nationally developed mathematics, science, and technology standards and the vision of teaching and learning implied by these standards (Chapter 2). Chapter 3 suggests a Framework for conceptualizing the influence on student learning of such national-level standards. The Framework identifies three key components of the education system—curriculum, teacher development, and assessment and accountability—as "channels" through which nationally promulgated reform ideas might move enroute to classrooms, describing ways that elements within each channel may affect teaching and learning.

The Framework is designed to address two overarching questions: *How has the system responded to the introduction of nationally developed standards?* and *What are the consequences for student learning?* The overarching questions may be explored by analyzing each Framework component in terms of several more specific queries: How are nationally developed standards being received and interpreted? What actions have been taken? What has changed as a result? Who has been affected and how? Rather than providing answers, this document embeds those questions within an analytical Framework to guide others in seeking answers.

Chapters 4 through 6 examine the three Framework channels identified in Chapter 3. These chapters address: the curriculum—what shapes what is taught to whom (Chapter 4); teacher development—how teachers learn what and how to teach (Chapter 5); and assessment and accountability—what kinds of assessments are used and for what purposes (Chapter 6). Each chapter suggests where the influence of standards may be found within that channel and employs Framework questions to suggest areas of potentially useful investigation.

Chapter 7 addresses public, professional, and political communities, focusing on their possible involvement in standards-based changes. Influence from such external sources might flow into the education system and consequently affect the channels and what happens to teaching and learning in the classroom.

Finally, Chapter 8 suggests how the Framework might be used to situate existing studies within the educational terrain that is relevant to the standards, to critically examine claims and inferences advanced by these studies, and to generate hypotheses to be explored through future investigations.

CHAPTER 2

STANDARDS FOR MATHEMATICS, SCIENCE, AND TECHNOLOGY EDUCATION

The term "standards" conveys different meanings to different people. For many members of the general public and for the education policy community, "standards" focus on outcomes and imply "a mechanism by which to hold schools accountable for what students learn" (Raizen, 1998, p. 73). In such cases, specific levels of performance relative to standards are defined, and assessments are designed to measure student progress toward attaining those standards. Assessment results may then be used as part of an accountability system, as a professional development tool to provide feedback to teachers, or to inform policy decisions. Ravitch (1995, p. 13) points out that policy makers and others also use "opportunity-to-learn, or school delivery, standards" in regard to "the availability of programs, staff, and other resources that schools, districts, and states provide so that students are able to meet challenging content and performance standards."

To many educators, a "standard" is a statement describing what a person should know or be able to do. That use of "standard" is often called a "content standard." In *Testing, Teaching, and Learning* (National Research Council [NRC], 1999f) a content standard is defined as setting "expectations for learning for all students." The National Council of Teachers of Mathematics (NCTM, 1989), the National Research Council (NRC, 1996), and International Technology Education Association (ITEA, 2000) use the word standard in a broader sense, including not just content standards, but also standards for teaching, assessment, and professional development as well as other standards to support their enactment.

THE CONTEXT IN WHICH STANDARDS EVOLVED

For mathematics and science education, several reform periods occurred during the first half of the twentieth century, as educators attempted to improve education for an ever-widening school audience (Hurd, 1960; NCTM, 1970). Then, in 1957, the Soviet Union's launching of Sputnik captured national attention and stimulated public pressure to upgrade U.S. science and mathematics education, with particular emphasis on increasing the pool of U.S. scientists and engineers capable of surpassing the Soviet achievement (Hurd and Gallagher, 1968; Raizen, 1991). While those efforts were at least partially successful, teacher, parent, and public discomfort with some of the emerging curricula contributed to counter-reforms that followed two quite different pathways. One led "back to basics," while the other sought more socially relevant instructional approaches (Raizen, 1991; DeBoer, 1991).

In 1983, *A Nation at Risk* declared that "...the educational foundations of our society are presently being eroded by a rising tide of mediocrity that threatens our very future as a Nation and a people" (National Commission on Excellence in Education, 1983, p. 5). The document called for higher student expectations and equitable treatment of all learners, improvement in teacher preparation and the teaching profession, leadership by educators and elected officials, and increased fiscal support from citizens. It stimulated new thinking within the U.S. mathematics and science communities about how to address changing societal needs and, consequently, about the need to prepare a mathematically and scientifically literate population for the future. Later publications—such as *A Nation Prepared: Teachers for the 21st Century* (Carnegie Forum on Education and the Economy, 1986)—reemphasized that educational reforms must provide equitable opportunities for all students.

States responded in the 1980s by developing new curriculum guidelines, frameworks, standards, and testing programs (e.g., Education Commission of the States, 1983; Armstrong, Davis, Odden, and Gallagher, 1988; Davis and Armstrong, 1990). By the end of the decade, the NCTM Standards and the American Association for the Advancement of Science's (AAAS) *Science for All Americans* (1989) articulated a national direction for teaching and learning in mathematics, science, and technology. President George H.W. Bush convened the first National Education Summit to discuss national educational goals with state governors (Miller, 1989). Discussions initiated at the summit transmuted into discussions about national education standards (National Governors Association [NGA], 1990; Fuhrman and Elmore, 1994), and in 1990, the National Education Goals Panel was formed.

Standards were soon embraced as a way to improve education and became the consensus view among state and national policy makers, crossing partisan lines (National Council on Education Standards and Testing, 1992). "Systemic reform" was conceptualized as a strategy to align reform activities across all components of the education system, rather than pursuing isolated changes in parts of the system (Smith and O'Day, 1991; O'Day and Smith, 1993).

During the 1990s, states and school districts adapted the nationally developed standards in various ways (Humphrey, Anderson, Marsh, Marder, and Shields, 1997; Council of Chief State School Officers [CCSSO], 1997). Many states initiated additional efforts aimed at improving education, and, for many reformers, the term "systemic reform" became synonymous with "standards-based reform."

The mathematics, science, and technology teaching and learning promoted by the NCTM, NRC, and ITEA standards documents reflect the reform period within which they were developed. The vision they describe represents a departure from common patterns of practice (Weiss, 1978, 1987; Weiss et al., 1994; Stake and Easley, 1978; Stigler and Hiebert, 1999). The nationally developed NCTM, NRC, and ITEA standards are addressed in the following sections, with emphasis on their scope, interrelationships, and commonality of vision.

DEVELOPING NATIONAL STANDARDS IN MATHEMATICS

In 1985, NCTM funded a group of its members—including teachers, researchers, and higher education representatives involved in mathematics teacher education—to create standards for K-12 mathematics. The resulting *Curriculum and Evaluation Standards for School Mathematics* (NCTM, 1989) provided classroom teachers, school mathematics coordinators, and curriculum developers with a vision and guidance for shaping content, instruction, and assessment within K-12 mathematics programs. NCTM standards called for content changes that reflected changing needs in an increasingly technological world, such as the inclusion of statistics, probability, and discrete mathematics in K-12 curricula. The document also specified standards for problem-solving, communicating, reasoning, and making connections—that is, portraying mathematics as something that is done, not just a body of material to be memorized.

NCTM followed the release of curriculum standards with publication of *Professional Standards for Teaching Mathematics* (1991) and *Assessment Standards for School Mathematics* (1995). These documents emphasized that, in addition to appropriate student learning goals, appropriate teaching and assessment were critical components of an effective mathematics program.

In 1995, in response to what had been learned since the publication of the first set of standards, new research in teaching and learning, and the increased sophistication and power of technology, NCTM began work on updating the mathematics standards. The new document, *Principles and Standards for School Mathematics*

BOX 2-1 Basic Principles and Features of *Principles and Standards for School Mathematics*

This document is intended to (p. 6):

- set forth a comprehensive and coherent set of goals for mathematics for all students from prekindergarten through grade 12 that will orient curricular, teaching, and assessment efforts during the next decades;
- serve as a resource for teachers, education leaders, and policymakers to use in examining and improving the quality of mathematics instructional programs;
- guide the development of curriculum frameworks, assessments, and instructional materials;
- stimulate ideas and ongoing conversations at the national, provincial or state, and local levels about how best to help students gain a deep understanding of important mathematics.

The six principles for school mathematics address overarching themes (p. 11):

- ***Equity.*** Excellence in mathematics education requires equity—high expectations and strong support for all students.
- ***Curriculum.*** A curriculum is more than a collection of activities: it must be coherent, focused on important mathematics, and well articulated across the grades.
- ***Teaching.*** Effective mathematics teaching requires understanding what students know and need to learn and then challenging and supporting them to learn it well.
- ***Learning.*** Students must learn mathematics with understanding, actively building new knowledge from experience and prior knowledge.
- ***Assessment.*** Assessment should support the learning of important mathematics and furnish useful information to both teachers and students.
- ***Technology.*** Technology is essential in teaching and learning mathematics; it influences the mathematics that is taught and enhances students' learning.

SOURCE: NCTM, 2000.

(NCTM, 2000), under the umbrella of goals and principles, focuses on content expectations along with instruction and assessment and devotes increased attention to the vertical (pre-K-12) development of important mathematical ideas (see Box 2-1).[1]

[1]Several publications document the development, expected applications, and dissemination of NCTM mathematics standards, and their use in developing state standards (NRC and NCTM, 1997; Romberg, 1998; Kirst and Bird, 1997; McLeod et al., 1996; Humphrey et al., 1997; CCSSO, 1997; Weiss et al., 1994).

DEVELOPING NATIONAL STANDARDS IN SCIENCE

As with the mathematics standards developed by NCTM, efforts leading to development of science standards were initiated by educators. AAAS's Project 2061 began efforts to identify desired learning goals in the mid-1980s. As its title implies, *Science for All Americans* (AAAS, 1989) reflected the consensus of much of the scientific community regarding a common core of learnings for everyone in science, mathematics, and technology. Then, based on cognitive research and the expertise of teachers and teacher leaders, *Benchmarks for Science Literacy* (AAAS, 1993) described how those core concepts can be introduced and developed within the grade-level spans of K-12 schooling. In 1989, the National Science Teachers Association (NSTA) started its Scope, Sequence, and Coordination project, which sought to delineate a multigrade sequencing of concepts across scientific disciplines within the secondary-school curriculum (NSTA, 1992). In 1991, the NRC agreed to coordinate development of national science education standards, supported by funding from the National Science Foundation (NSF), U.S. Department of Education, National Aeronautics and Space Administration (NASA), and National Institutes of Health. The *National Science Education Standards* (NRC, 1996), informed by the earlier work of NCTM, AAAS, and NSTA, emerged as the central product of that collaborative effort.

Again, consistent with intentions of the mathematics standards, NRC standards offered a vision of science education for all students, including what they should know, understand, and be able to do within particular K-12 grade intervals. In addition to physical, life, earth, and space science concepts, the content standards addressed science as inquiry, unifying concepts and processes (such as systems and the nature of models), science and technology, science in personal and social perspectives, and the history and nature of science. Furthermore, the document takes a systemic perspective, including standards that address science teaching,

BOX 2-2 Basic Principles and Features of *National Science Education Standards*

Purpose (p. 17):

Define scientific literacy
- Principles and Definitions (Chapter 2)
- Content Standards (Chapter 6)

Provide guidance for teachers and other science educators
- Teaching Standards (Chapter 3)
- Assessment Standards (Chapter 5)
- Professional Development Standards (Chapter 4)

Clarify the responsibility of policy makers and the community
- Program Standards (Chapter 7)
- System Standards (Chapter 8)

Principles (p. 19):

- Science is for all students.
- Learning science is an active process.
- School science reflects the intellectual and cultural traditions that characterize the practice of contemporary science.
- Improving science education is part of systemic education reform.

SOURCE: NRC, 1996.

professional development, and assessment at classroom, district, state, and national levels, as well as standards that address the necessary components of a comprehensive school science program, and policies and resources deemed necessary from all components of the education system to attain science literacy for all students (see Box 2-2).[2]

[2]Numerous publications document the development, intended uses, and dissemination of the *National Science Education Standards* (Raizen, 1998; NRC and NCTM, 1997; Bybee, 1997; Collins, 1997; NRC, 1997; Kirst and Bird, 1997; Humphrey et al., 1997; CCSSO, 1997).

DEVELOPING STANDARDS FOR TECHNOLOGICAL LITERACY

In 1994, ITEA initiated the Technology for All Americans Project, funded by NSF and NASA, to promote the study of technology and attainment of technological literacy for all citizens. The project, through release of *Technology for All Americans: A Rationale and Structure for the Study of Technology* (ITEA, 1996), defined what a technologically literate person should know and be able to do. The document argues that technological literacy will enable all Americans to become informed decision makers and participate fully in a technological society. It also defines the processes, knowledge, and contexts that constitute the study of technology, and describes how technology should be integrated into the K-12 curriculum.

The project's second phase led to release of *Standards for Technological Literacy: Content for the Study of Technology* (ITEA, 2000). That document defines technological literacy, distinguishing what all students should know and understand about technology from what they should be able to do (e.g., apply a design process to solve a technological problem). The standards, organized within four grade-level ranges, address the nature of technology; technology and society; design; abilities for a technological world; and the designed world (see Box 2-3).

ITEA received third-phase funding from NSF and NASA to develop assessment, program, and professional development standards to complement and guide implementation of the technology content standards.[3]

COMMONALITIES ACROSS THE MATHEMATICS, SCIENCE, AND TECHNOLOGY STANDARDS

The standards for mathematics, science, and technology share a number of key characteristics, starting with affirmation of the

[3]Several articles describe the development of the Standards for Technological Literacy, their dissemination, and intended uses (e.g., Dugger, 2000, 2001; Wulf, 2000).

BOX 2-3 Basic Principles and Features of *Standards for Technological Literacy: Content for the Study of Technology*

Technology Content Standards is designed as a guide for educating students in developing technological literacy. Technological literacy is the ability to use, manage, assess, and understand technology. A technologically literate person understands, in increasingly sophisticated ways that evolve over time, what technology is, how it is created, and how it shapes society, and in turn is shaped by society. He or she will be able to hear a story about technology on television or read it in the newspaper and evaluate the information in the story intelligently, put that information in context, and form an opinion based on that information. A technologically literate person will be comfortable with and objective about technology, neither scared of it nor infatuated with it (pp. 9–10).

Technology is defined as the modification of the natural environment in order to satisfy human needs and wants (p. 7). The Technology Content Standards lay out what should be learned and accomplished by each student in the study of technology at four levels (p. 13).

Basic features (p.13):

- It offers a common set of expectations for what students in technology laboratory-classrooms should learn.
- It is developmentally appropriate for students.
- It provides a basis for developing meaningful, relevant, and articulated curricula at the local, state, and provincial levels.
- It promotes content connections with other fields of study in grades K-12.

SOURCE: ITEA, 2000.

importance of increased expectations, opportunities, and achievement of all students, including groups largely bypassed historically, such as girls and ethnic and language minorities. All three sets of standards call on teachers to recognize the rich diversity students bring to classrooms—their linguistic backgrounds, cultures, and world views, as well as their prior knowledge and beliefs about scientific phenomena, mathematical concepts, and technological innovations—and provide opportunities for all students to learn.

The nationally developed mathematics, science, and technology standards offer a vision of what literate citizens should know and be able to do within their respective subject areas, along with descriptions of the teaching practices, professional development, resources, assessment practices, and support needed to achieve such literacy. All three sets of standards articulate a common vision for improving student learning—a vision that emphasizes understanding of basic concepts and "big ideas" in each subject area, acquisition of useful skills, engagement in inquiry-based learning, and coherent articulation of learning opportunities across all grade levels. The standards call for instruction that actively engages students in learning and that provides all students with opportunities to learn challenging mathematics, science, and technology concepts and skills. The standards also call for students to be able to use their knowledge, skills, and understanding to make decisions and participate productively in society, as well as to solve problems and communicate their thinking and reasoning to others (NCTM, 1995, p. 11; NRC, 1996, pp. 22-23; ITEA, 2000, p. 9-10). All three sets of standards deliberately leave specific curricular decisions to state and local officials, including assignment of specific content to each grade level (NCTM, 2000, p. 7; NRC, 1996, pp. 111-112; ITEA, 2000, p. 200).

The NCTM, NRC, and ITEA standards call for changes not only in what students learn, but also in how that content is taught. According to the national standards documents, teachers should have deep understanding of the science, mathematics, and technology content they teach; recognize and address common student preconceptions; design classroom experiences that actively engage students in building their understanding; emphasize the use and application of what is learned; and use assessment as an integral part of instruction. Teachers should listen carefully to students' ideas; recognize and respond to student diversity; facilitate and encourage student discussions; model the skills and strategies of scientific inquiry, mathematical problem-solving, and technological innovation and ingenuity; and help students cultivate those skills and behaviors. In so doing, teachers should establish a classroom climate that supports learning; encourages respect for the ideas of others; and values curiosity, skepticism, and diverse viewpoints. In addition, teachers should participate in ongoing planning and development of mathematics, science, and technology programs in their schools and seek and promote professional-growth opportunities for themselves and their colleagues (NCTM, 1991, pp. 20-22; NRC, 1996, pp. 27-54).

In short, teachers are expected to be well-versed in the content they teach and masterful in their uses of appropriate pedagogy. One group of commentators described the instructional practices advocated by the national standards this way:

> There is no well-defined set of techniques that will reliably produce high levels of student performance when applied in a routine manner. Rather, to teach in a manner consistent with the new vision, a teacher would not only have to be extraordinarily knowledgeable, but would also need to have a certain sort of motivation or will: the disposition to engage daily in a persistent, directed search for the combination of tasks, materials, questions, and responses that will enable her students to learn each new idea. In other words, she must be results-oriented, intently focused on what her students are actually learning rather than simply on her own routines for "covering" the curriculum. Her knowledge and skill are valuable resources, but judgment and continuous invention are required to turn these resources into effective performance. (Thompson, Spillane, and Cohen, 1994, p. 4)

The NCTM, NRC, and ITEA standards embody a vision of what professionals in each subject area believe is needed to improve the teaching and learning in their respective subject areas. However, in attempts to understand the influence of these standards, it is important to consider what must happen within the education system to realize that vision. The next chapter examines the system within which that desired teaching and learning must occur and identifies key interactions among that system's components. That analysis leads to a framework to guide investigations regarding the possible influence of nationally developed standards upon and within that system and—most critically—on classroom teaching and learning.

CHAPTER 3

A FRAMEWORK FOR INVESTIGATING THE INFLUENCE OF EDUCATION STANDARDS

This chapter provides a Framework for identifying and judging possible influences of nationally developed standards on what teachers do and what students learn. The chapter begins with a general overview of the education system within which teaching and learning occur. It then describes key channels through which education can be influenced and ways that reform ideas (such as standards) may travel through the system. The chapter closes by suggesting a Framework that highlights relevant facets of the education system and frames queries that need to be addressed when dealing with two overarching questions: *How has the system responded to the introduction of nationally developed mathematics, science, and technology standards?* and *What are the consequences for student learning?*

AN OVERVIEW OF THE U.S. EDUCATION SYSTEM

The United States education system is large, diverse, and complex. Approximately 2.7 million teachers are responsible for the education of more than 47 million pupils in nearly 90,000 public schools; another 6 million students attend private schools (National Center for Education Statistics [NCES], 2000b). Such aggregated nationwide data, however, fail to reveal the variation and increasing diversity of student bodies located in different regions of the country—in rural, suburban, and urban areas, and in affluent and impoverished communities. Student populations in urban schools are particularly diverse. A large majority of urban students have non-white ethnic backgrounds, and increasing numbers are recent immigrants not yet proficient in English (NCES, 1997c; 1999).

The U.S. teacher population also brings an array of different knowledge bases, expectations, cultural backgrounds, and beliefs to classrooms. Since nearly 90 percent of U.S. K-12 teachers are white (NCES, 2000b), teachers in some schools are demographically quite different than their students.

The individual classrooms within which teachers and students interact constitute the core of the education system. At the same time, what happens in a classroom is significantly affected by decisions made in other layers of this loosely coupled system. First there is the school as an educational unit; setting expectations in certain content areas, the principal, department chairs, or team leaders can affect beliefs about teaching and learning priorities. They can also establish a climate that encourages or discourages particular pedagogical approaches, collegial interactions, or inservice programs (Talbert and McLaughlin, 1993; McLaughlin, 1993; Little 1993). A school's level of commitment to equity and to providing opportunities for all students to learn the same core content can influence how students are scheduled into classes, which teachers are assigned to teach particular classes, and how instructional resources are identified and allocated.

In the next layer of the system, school districts are responsible for ensuring implementation of state and federal education policies, and often create additional, local education policy. District leaders set instructional priorities, provide instructional guidance, create incentive structures, and may influence the willingness and capacity of schools and teachers to explore and implement different instructional techniques.

The state level is a particularly important one for schools. In the United States, states are constitutionally responsible for elementary and secondary education, and they play major roles in funding and regulating education, providing nearly half of all public school revenues (NCES, 2000a). Each state is responsible for developing and administering its own policies for standards, curriculum, materials selection and adoption, teacher licensure, student assessment, and educational accountability. Across states, the authority of schools and districts to enact policy varies considerably. In states with "local control," more power resides at the district level than is found in states with centralized control.

Although the federal government contributes less than 10 percent of all funds invested by states and local districts in education (U.S. Department of Education [USDoE], 2000a), it influences education at all levels through a combination of regulations, public advocacy, and monetary incentives. For example, the USDoE creates mandates for serving special-needs students, provides aid for districts serving disadvantaged students, and distributes funds to support professional development (through Title I and Title II of the Elementary and Secondary Education Act). In addition, the National Science Foundation and other federal agencies award competitive grants that address targeted educational priorities in science, mathematics, and technology education.

ONE VIEW OF THE EDUCATION SYSTEM

Based on research, interactions with practitioners in the field, and members' own experiences, the authoring Committee has chosen to represent the U.S. education system as shown in Figure 3-1. The figure highlights the layers of governance described earlier in this chapter and identifies three main routes or "channels" through which national reform ideas might flow to various layers of the system and eventually influence teaching and learning. It also includes the social and political contexts within which the U.S. education system operates. Other factors, such as organizational development, could have been selected as system components, but the Committee agreed that the elements identified in Figure 3-1 are most relevant to tracing potential effects of nationally developed standards on the education system—and, in particular, on student learning.

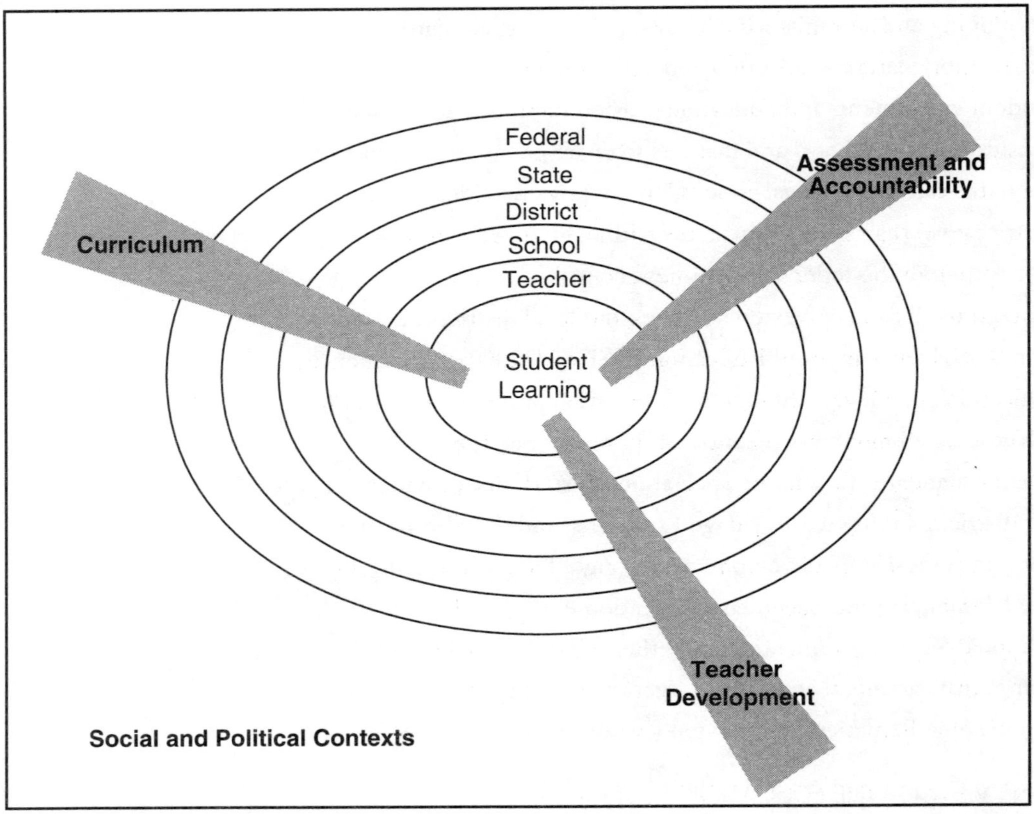

FIGURE 3-1 The Layers of Education Governance and Channels Through Which Reform Might Flow

As reforms (such as standards) enter the education system and traverse one or more "channels," they may affect policies, programs, and practices within various jurisdictional layers. The channels are:

- *Curriculum.* Mandates and resources from legislative bodies, and decisions and developmental work by teachers, school and district curriculum coordinators, state agencies, curriculum development organizations, and textbook publishers all collectively define what teachers should teach and students should learn. Nationally developed standards, as well as state and local standards, typically play roles in this process, and thus may help to define the content of instruction.

- *Teacher Development.* School districts, institutions of higher education, state agencies, and other entities recruit, prepare, license, and evaluate teachers, as well as provide an array of opportunities for continued professional learning. Nationally developed standards can inform these processes in many ways, influencing the content and expectations for teacher preparation and for their career-long professional growth.
- *Assessment and Accountability.* Student assessment practices—created by teachers, district or state agencies, assessment developers, postsecondary institutions, and others—establish ways that student learning is monitored, and, in so doing, may operationally define the classroom content that matters most. Based on assessment results, accountability mechanisms often establish consequences for students, teachers, and schools. Nationally developed standards may define the content domain that assessments address, as well as prompt development of new forms of assessment.

Standards may also have an impact on education's social and political contexts, spurring those outside the education system to influence, both directly and indirectly, what happens in classrooms. For example, what parents and other members of the public, their political representatives, the media, and relevant professional organizations say and do can influence the practice of public education. How stakeholders outside the education system understand and interpret standards may therefore influence how—and whether—standards ultimately cause changes in classroom teaching and learning.

THE ELEMENTS OF THE FRAMEWORK

Based on the Committee's view of the education system, described above, the Committee developed a Framework that consists, first, of a conceptual map that shows the contextual forces

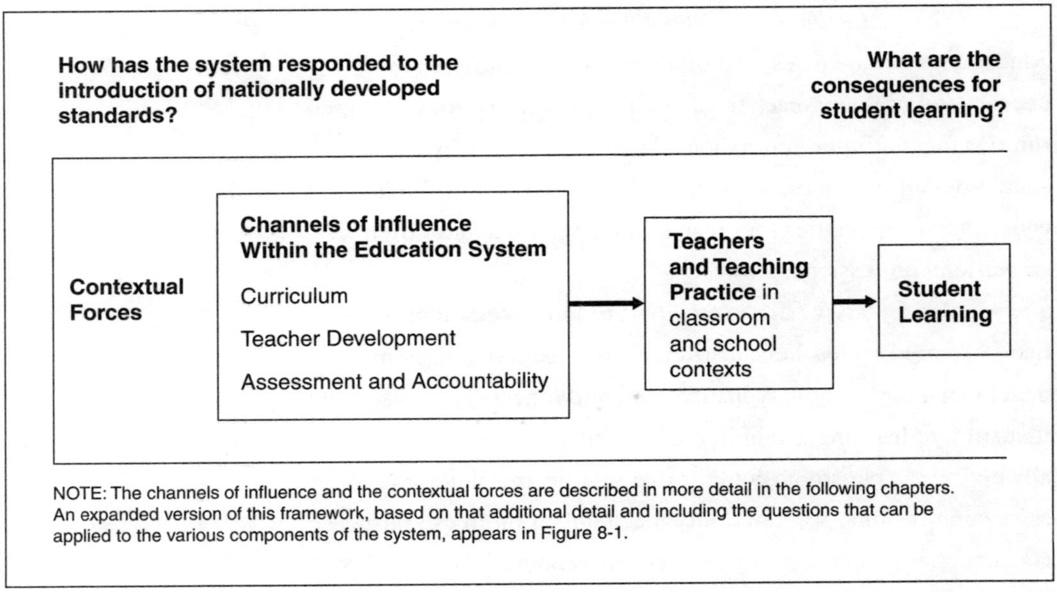

FIGURE 3-2 A Conceptual Map for Investigating the Influence of Nationally Developed Standards for Mathematics, Science, and Technology Education

and channels through which nationally developed standards may influence teachers and student learning (see Figure 3-2).

Second, the Framework includes a set of guiding questions that can be applied to various policies, programs, and practices within the system and to outside influences that may affect the system (see Figure 3-3).

As configured, the Framework provides conceptual guideposts for those attempting to trace the influence of nationally developed mathematics, science, and technology standards and to gauge the magnitude or direction of that influence on the education system and on student learning. In other words, the Framework is intended to guide inquiries within the education territory encompassed by the map.

As is true for all models, the system represented in the Framework is greatly simplified. Those simplifications, however, should not obscure these important realities:

Within the education system and in its context—	**Among teachers who have been exposed to nationally developed standards—**	**Among students who have been exposed to standards-based practice—**
• How are nationally developed standards being received and interpreted? • What actions have been taken in response? • What has changed as a result? • What components of the system have been affected and how?	• How have they received and interpreted those standards? • What actions have they taken in response? • What, if anything, about their classroom practice has changed? • Who has been affected and how?	• How have student learning and achievement changed? • Who has been affected and how?

FIGURE 3-3 A Set of Guiding Questions for Investigating the Influences of Nationally Developed Standards

- The channels of influence are complex and interactive, both with other components of the education system and among different levels of jurisdiction. For example, changes in the curriculum framework of a state may affect a district's teacher-development program.
- The time needed for the influences of any set of standards to traverse the system may be long. One of the principal players in the development of standards wrote that the estimate of "a decade or longer" to implement the standards was "modest" (Collins, 1997).
- Reform ideas may be altered or ignored for various reasons (including prior beliefs and ongoing debate) as they work their way through the education system. Thus, nationally developed standards may stimulate the intended changes, create a backlash, or result in no changes at all.
- Local, state, and regional variability within the U.S. education system all imply that teachers and students are likely to be influenced differently within different locales, depending on available resources, participant backgrounds, and other factors.

Although this Framework has been developed specifically to guide thinking regarding nationally developed mathematics, science, and technology standards, it is intended to support comparable considerations for any set of education standards. In short, the Framework is designed to guide inquiry into the influence of standards on various parts and levels of the education system. Those investigations may be centered on one or more of these key questions:

How are nationally developed standards being received and interpreted? Because the vision expressed in the standards for student learning, teaching practice, and system behavior is conveyed through broadly framed statements, it is subject to interpretation. Accordingly, individuals throughout the system will necessarily engage in various forms of sense-making, drawing on prior beliefs, knowledge, and priorities, as they give educational and operational meaning to the standards (Spillane and Callahan, 2000). Thus, to understand anything about the influence of standards, answers to this first central question are needed. The answers will reveal much about how expectations embedded in nationally developed standards are understood, and whether they are accepted, rejected, or altered in that interpretive process.

What actions have been taken? What have curriculum developers, teacher educators, and assessment designers done in response to standards? Actions taken by individuals or entities with respect to the standards will depend on their interpretations, and on their capacities and determination. Variations in resources, professional expertise, structural features, working cultures, and values will affect their motivation and ability to implement nationally developed standards in some form or other. Enactment of standards represents an unfolding story of reform intentions interacting with the multiple contexts within which teachers work and learners learn (Talbert and McLaughlin, 1993). That story will unfold differently in particular states and localities depending on what educators support, seek, and are able to accomplish. As decades of research on policy and program implementation attest (Anderson, 1996; Anderson and Helms, 2001; McLaughlin, 1987, 1991), it is likely that enactments of nationally developed standards will take on very different forms as implementation proceeds.

What has changed as a result? What new policies, programs, or practices can be attributed to the influence of standards? Attempts to implement national standards, whether faithful to their original intentions or to alternative interpretations, do not guarantee educational improvement. Furthermore, as the Framework implies, incorporation of standards into one part of the system may or may not lead to programs and practices in other parts of the system that mirror the intent of the nationally developed standards. Ultimately, what matters is how student learning is affected—or to be more precise, whether standards-based changes in the education system and in teaching practice have led to improvements in student learning.

Who has been affected and how? In specific terms, how has the learning of students who have been exposed to standards-based practice been affected, and do these effects vary across groups or types of students? For the student population, or subsets of it, do effects on learning represent an improvement? Substantial inequities continue to be documented within U.S. education in general (e.g., Darling-Hammond, 2000) and within mathematics, science, and technology education in particular (National Commission on Mathematics and Science Teaching for the 21st Century, 2000; Martin et al., 2001; Mullis et al., 2001). Thus, it is entirely possible that nationally developed standards or other educational interventions may engender practices that differentially benefit (or harm) some segments of the student population, or that benefit some schools or communities more than others. Nationally developed mathematics, science, and technology standards explicitly call for reform in policies and practice leading to literacy for *all* students. It is imperative that investigations of the influence of nationally developed standards address this critical question when examining particular elements of the system and when gathering evidence regarding student learning.

If these four central questions within the Framework are used in the context of particular investigations, both producers and consumers of research can acquire important insights into possible benefits and limitations of nationally developed standards.

The next four chapters provide more detail regarding the channels and outside forces through which standards may influence the education system. Each chapter starts with a brief overview of that part of the system, examines ways in which nationally developed standards might stimulate either positive or negative changes, and identifies places to look for evidence of any impact standards may have had. The final chapter examines ways in which the Framework can be applied to develop understanding of the influence of standards in the U.S. education system.

CHAPTER 4

CURRICULUM AS A CHANNEL OF INFLUENCE: WHAT SHAPES WHAT IS TAUGHT TO WHOM?

Policies, practices, and resources of the federal government, states, districts, schools, and teachers all play roles in influencing the development of curriculum and instructional programs, their implementation, and thus, what is actually taught to particular students. Exploring curriculum as a channel of influence means addressing:

- Policy decisions about curriculum and resources to support the curriculum,
- Development of instructional materials and programs, and
- Processes and criteria for selecting instructional materials.

CURRICULUM IN THE EDUCATION SYSTEM

Implications of Policy Decisions

Many states play prominent roles in determining public school curricula—the content outlines and sequences of topics that, as a whole, specify what mathematics, science, and technology content students are to learn. This state role has expanded considerably as state standards, curriculum frameworks, and accountability measures have emerged as key strategies in the search for educational improvements (National Science Foundation [NSF], 1996; Massell, Kirst and Hoppe, 1997; U.S. Department of Education [USDoE], 1999; *Education Week*, 2001). State education agencies may establish high-school completion requirements or exit exams, which, in effect, often define the core content students are expected to learn.

Some state policies directly address the intended curriculum and the resources needed to enact it, as well as other facets of the education system that affect curriculum, such as regulations governing remedial or special education programs. State policies addressing student access to classroom laboratories and information technologies also can influence what is taught. Accreditation protocols, including compliance reviews of federally funded programs, place increasing demands on schools to clearly define and support mathematics, science, and technology content congruent with state learning standards and frameworks.

The federal government influences the school curriculum mainly through policy decisions that affect resource allocations. For example, NSF provides funds for science, mathematics, and technology materials-development projects. USDoE also supports programs that may implicitly or explicitly encourage particular visions of mathematics, science, and technology education, as well as particular strategies for attaining these visions, for example, through enactment of the Eisenhower Professional Development Program (Dwight D. Eisenhower Mathematics and Science Education Act, PL 103-382). On occasion, federal government officials make use of the "bully pulpit" to issue direct statements about curriculum. For example, fueled by concerns about U.S. student achievement results in the Third International Mathematics and Science Study (National Center for Education Statistics [NCES], 1996), the Secretary of Education emphasized the importance of algebra and geometry instruction at earlier ages for all students (Riley, 2000).

School district policies and practices such as graduation requirements and course offerings also affect the range and depth of science, mathematics, and technology content in schools. These policies, in turn, are influenced by community values and culture, including traditions and expectations regarding what schools should teach and what resources should be allocated to mathematics, science, and technology education (Shepard, 2000). In addition, school-based decisions about class scheduling and the time allotted for science, technology, or mathematics instruction can influence the quality of the programs offered to students (Council of Chief State School Officers [CCSSO], 1999b). For example, programmatic "tracks"—combined with expectations about what particular students can or should learn, and what should be taught to whom—often reflect school or district level policy (Oakes, Ormseth, Bell, and Camp, 1990; White, Porter, Gamoran and Smithson, 1996).

The curriculum channel is linked to the other components of the education system in multiple ways. Teacher development programs, the use of assessment and accountability to spur educational reform, and public influence on policy decisions may directly affect the school curriculum. These factors will be addressed in later chapters.

Development of Instructional Materials and Programs

Instructional materials represent the resources that teachers use to develop student understanding of subject-specific concepts and skills in the enactment of the curriculum. Such materials include textbooks, workbooks, laboratory manuals, manipulatives such as three-dimensional solids, laboratory supplies and equipment, videos, laser discs, CDs, software, and websites. Developed by many different entities, instructional materials often become critical, defining components of instructional programs (CCSSO, 2000; Weiss, 1991; Stake and Easley, 1978). In particular, commercial publishing firms with K-12 divisions dedicated to producing and selling school textbooks are central players in shaping what most teachers teach (Woodward and Elliot, 1990; Tyson, 1997). Educational material production is "big business"—in 1999, revenues from K-12 instructional materials of the top five publishers totaled over $3.3 billion (Walsh, 2000). Thus, although publishers can and do produce materials in response to particular educational changes, decisions to invest in such development are always tempered by estimates of the potential demand for materials supporting those changes. Accordingly, curricular content specified as important by textbook adoption policies in large states has great influence on the content of commercially available texts (Tyson, 1997).

Instructional materials are also produced by entities other than publishing companies. Federal agencies and other grant-awarding sources often support nonprofit organizations and educators at universities or school districts in producing discipline-specific instructional materials and programs. Teachers may also create some of their own materials individually and with peers, sometimes in response to school or district curriculum frameworks and sometimes based on their own views of what is important for students to learn or based on materials they encounter at professional meetings.

Teacher-support materials developed by commercial publishers or districts, designed to assist teachers as they begin to implement new programs and materials or attempt to integrate technology into their curriculum, are key elements in the curricular system. In part to address concerns about underprepared teachers, demands have increased for such materials to accompany student materials, offering support to teachers in helping them to understand what to teach and how to teach it (National Research Council [NRC], 1999e). Another consideration is the well-documented fact that the enacted curriculum is often different than the intended curriculum (Robitaille et al., 1993; NCES, 1996; Ferrini-Mundy and Schram, 1997). What teachers actually elect to teach and to whom may reflect their own interpretation of the curriculum, as well as their school and classroom environment.

Selection Mechanisms

A wide range of forces shape the processes for selecting instructional materials used in schools. These events are largely dependent on a district's financial status and its current educational focus (NRC, 1999e). The timing of textbook adoptions is often linked to school funding cycles; the purchase of resource materials to support the curriculum often correlates to textbook-adoption cycles but may also be subject to uncertain budgets. It is not uncommon for an adopted textbook to remain in use for five to eight—or even ten—years; a text selected in 1995 could still be in use in 2005.

Teachers sometimes select materials that conform to their own beliefs about teaching, despite district curriculum guidelines or the changing nature of the subject (Grossman and Stodolsky, 1995; CCSSO, 2000). Decisions about instructional materials may be influenced by public and community preferences or by achievement results on high-stakes assessments (Massell, Kirst, and Hoppe, 1997; Battista, 1999; Anderson and Helms, 2001; Becker and Jacob, 2000). Decisions may also be influenced by endorsements of federal agencies (USDoE's Mathematics and Science Expert Panel, 2000) or by curriculum evaluations published by nongovernmental groups such as the American Association for the Advancement of Science (AAAS) Project 2061, the Mathematically Correct, or the American Institute of Biological Sciences (AIBS)(AAAS, 2000; Clopton et al., 1998; Morse and the AIBS Review Team, 2001).

In about twenty states, including many in the South and West, a statewide selection process for instructional materials, usually guided by state specifications for student learning, leads to lists of state-approved textbooks, with one or more titles specified for each discipline and grade level (Weiss, 1991; Tyson 1997). Once a particular instructional program is placed on a state-adoption list, funds allocated by the state for instructional materials can be accessed by districts and schools to purchase that curricular program.

At the district level, the selection and purchase process for instructional materials is highly idiosyncratic. The nature of adoption mechanisms for instructional materials depends, in part, on the level of human and fiscal resources available to districts or schools. In some instances, a formal process specifies development and use of explicit criteria tied to district or state goals or linked to statewide assessments. In technology education, cross-discipline committees sometimes define the curriculum and ways in which technology will be implemented in classrooms, while in other cases the technology education departments make those choices and recommendations.

In summary, the selection and adoption of textbooks is closely related to state and district policies and funding procedures. In some instances, the availability and administration of financial resources directly affect how often schools and teachers adopt new textbooks, which schools and students have access to instructional resources to support the curriculum, which instructional resources are available for which teachers, and how teachers are supported in their use of such resources.

HOW STANDARDS MIGHT INFLUENCE CURRICULUM

Nationally developed standards describe the organization, balance, and presentation of important mathematics, science, and technology content. The standards intentionally do not prescribe a specific curriculum, but provide criteria for designing a curriculum framework or selecting instructional materials.

If standards are influencing what is taught to which students, then curriculum policy, the design and development of instructional materials, and the processes and criteria by which such materials are selected and implemented in classrooms would reflect the content described in the standards. Enacted policies and funded programs defining curriculum would align with those relating to standards-based instruction and assessment. State content standards would be consistent with content specified by the nationally developed standards, providing comprehensive guidance on what should be taught at each grade level, stimulating creation or adoption of curricular materials and textbooks at the local level that embody the standards' vision, and providing direction to needed curricular guidance and support. Graduation requirements would reinforce the curricular recommendations of the standards, and postsecondary institutions would recognize and accommodate students who successfully complete standards-based school programs.

If standards influenced the curriculum, both the intended and enacted curriculum would focus on mathematics, science, and technology learning goals specified in the standards; K-12 programs would be coordinated system-wide both within and across grades and aligned with the content as outlined in the standards documents. Schools, districts, and states would have an infrastructure supporting delivery of standards-based curricula in mathematics, science, and technology, including programs to support teachers' instructional needs in relation to those curricula. Instructional materials and textbooks would be developed by people who understand the standards, and that understanding would be reflected both in the content they include and the nature of the tasks they use to develop student knowledge of that content. Textbook adoption processes would be carried out by selection committees knowledgeable about standards-based materials. Textbook adoption criteria would be based on features congruent with the standards, such as inquiry-based learning, an emphasis on problem-solving, and an emphasis on conceptual understanding as well as skill development. Teachers would have appropriate resources for teaching standards-based curricula, including laboratory equipment and supplies, and support for learning to use them effectively.

Enrollment patterns in schools would reveal whether the vision expressed by the standards applies to all students. If standards are permeating the system, opportunities for taking challenging mathematics, science, and technology courses would be open to every student, and resources needed to implement a robust standards-based curriculum would be allocated in equitable ways. Dual-language materials would be available, as well as other resources designed to accommodate diverse learners to support the standards' focus on all students having access to opportunities to learn important mathematics, science, and technology concepts and skills.

THE CURRICULUM CHANNEL AND NATIONALLY DEVELOPED STANDARDS

The Framework questions (see Figure 3-3) offer guidance in studying the influence of standards on curriculum and instructional materials by focusing inquiry into matters such as:

- *How has the curriculum component of the education system responded to the introduction of nationally developed standards?*
- *How are these standards being received and interpreted by states as they work on their own standards, by curriculum developers who are designing instructional materials, by districts who are making decisions about K-12 curriculum programs and choosing instructional resources, and by teachers as they plan instruction and work with their students?*
- *What actions have been taken by states, district administrators, teachers, and textbook publishers to enact curriculum-related policies and practices that support the nationally developed standards?*
- *To what extent is the curriculum in schools and districts aligned with the nationally developed standards?*
- *To what extent are teachers teaching the content described in the standards and do they have the materials to do so in the ways the standards intended?*
- *To what extent are all students given access to curriculum consistent with the standards?*
- *And finally, who is being affected and how? Do all students have ample opportunity to learn the core content? Do they have adequate resources and support to aid them in learning that content?*

Studies that explore answers to such questions will inform the two overarching questions: *How has the system responded to the introduction of nationally developed mathematics, science, and technology standards?* and *What are the consequences for student learning?*

The next chapter addresses implications of another key channel of influence on the education system—teacher development. It represents a second major factor to be taken into account in evaluating the impact of nationally developed standards on student learning.

CHAPTER 5

TEACHER DEVELOPMENT AS A CHANNEL OF INFLUENCE: HOW DO TEACHERS LEARN WHAT AND HOW TO TEACH?

What is taught and learned in school depends not only on the curriculum, but also in very important ways on the classroom teachers who implement the curriculum. Teachers bring certain predispositions and beliefs to the classroom that influence their teaching. In addition, a variety of policies, mechanisms, practices, and resources shape the ways that teachers are prepared and how, over time, they are aided in their work.

The teacher development components within the system provide a channel through which nationally developed standards might influence how teachers learn to teach. This chapter explores three areas:

- Initial Preparation of Teachers
- Certification and Licensure
- Ongoing Professional Development

A range of other considerations are related to teachers' professional development including how schools and districts induct newly certified teachers into the profession; supervise, evaluate, and compensate teachers; provide administrative support and leadership; and establish safe work environments.

More general conditions surrounding schools also play roles in influencing who decides to teach, such as societal views of the teaching profession (affecting personal decisions about whether to enter the pool of teaching candidates), economic or social conditions in particular locales (affecting teachers' willingness to work in certain schools or districts), and demographics of the teaching profession (affecting whether students of different races and ethnic backgrounds can envision themselves working as teachers).

All of these conditions and elements constitute a web of influence on the work and careers of school teachers. Although that full set of conditions must be taken into account to represent the complete story, what follows concentrates on the aspects of teacher preparation and development that have the potential to be most directly influenced by nationally developed mathematics, science, and technology education standards.

TEACHER DEVELOPMENT IN THE EDUCATION SYSTEM

This section examines how prospective teachers learn mathematics, science, or technology content and pedagogy, how they become eligible for certification or licensure, and how their professional growth is encouraged during their teaching careers.

Teacher Preparation

There is broad agreement that teachers should be expert in subject matter content and pedagogical knowledge (National Research Council [NRC], 1999c; Shulman, 1986, 1987). For teachers entering the profession, such knowledge and skills are initially shaped by their exposure to mathematics, science, and technology content—and the ways those subjects are taught—prior to and during their formal teacher preparation program.

Both K-12 programs and courses completed at the college level provide early classroom experience with the subject areas that prospective teachers will later teach. How courses are presented conveys subtle messages to future teachers about the nature of the subject area, how that knowledge is acquired and tested, and how it should be taught to others. For example, learning calculus as an undergraduate through didactic lectures may predispose new mathematics teachers to teach in similar ways. Likewise, how courses are organized within a college physics department may influence how high school physics teachers organize coursework for their students. In recent years, some postsecondary institutions have been re-evaluating what (and how) content is taught to undergraduates; some institutions (e.g., Rothman and Narum, 2000) anticipate reforms in undergraduate education that may change the nature and quality of knowledge acquired by prospective teachers.[4]

Work experiences acquired by prospective school teachers may have also enriched and deepened their understanding of subjects they teach. This is especially true for mid-career professionals who leave laboratory or technical careers to enter teaching, but also may apply to younger teacher candidates who gain such experience through internships, summer employment, or other work and volunteer opportunities. Such "real world" experiences may provide them with valuable insights into the nature of science, mathematics, and technology.

Once enrolled in teacher preparation programs, prospective teachers are exposed to content and pedagogy through required subject matter courses and education courses.[5] Due to the organi-

---

[4] Several groups have issued recommendations regarding undergraduate courses required of prospective teachers. Recommendations from the Mathematics Education of Teachers Project (Conference Board on Mathematical Sciences, 2000) address both the nature of required mathematics courses (e.g., that they develop deep understanding of the mathematics undergraduates will be expected to teach) and the extent of those mathematics courses (ranging from nine semester hours for elementary teachers to a major for high school mathematics teachers). The National Science Teachers Association (NSTA, 1998) has issued comparable recommendations regarding science coursework for prospective teachers of science. In addition, the NRC Committee on Science and Mathematics Teacher Preparation (NRC, 2000) specifically recommends that the higher education community "assume greater responsibility for offering college-level courses that provide teachers with strong exposure to appropriate content and that model the kinds of pedagogical approaches appropriate for teaching that content" (p. 111).

[5] There are currently a number of mechanisms that enable individuals to enter teaching without participating in a conventional teacher preparation program, often associated with recruitment efforts intended to address teacher shortages. Alternative certification routes often involve some level of introduction to pedagogy, ranging from several "crash courses" during the summer before the candidate starts teaching to professional development extending over the first several years of a teaching career.

zation of higher education institutions, most subject matter preparation is delivered outside of schools of education. For instance, prospective science teachers complete courses in separate departments dedicated to various areas within the biological, earth, and physical sciences (Anderson and Mitchener, 1994). Faculty members in discipline-based departments may hold beliefs about teaching and learning science that differ from those held by education faculty. Coordination, communication, and common goals for teacher candidates are often difficult to accomplish across departments (or across colleges within a university) due to their physical separation, as well as to differing perspectives on education.

Prospective teachers also complete "methods" courses about the dynamics of classroom teaching and learning in particular content areas. Such courses, together with the modeling of pedagogical ideas by teacher educators and clinical experiences (e.g., supervised student teaching), constitute core experiences in mathematics, science, or technology teaching.

Certification and Licensure

Criteria for successful completion of a teacher preparation program and for securing a teaching certificate are influenced by professional accrediting bodies and state policy makers. These criteria define the base knowledge and skills expected of new teachers embarking on their professional work in classrooms. Associations such as the National Council for Accreditation of Teacher Education (NCATE) have set standards for accrediting teacher preparation programs. States employ NCATE or similar criteria in evaluating and approving undergraduate teacher preparation programs and implement accountability systems intended to ensure that institutions adhere to those criteria (Hirsch, Koppich, and Knapp, 2000).

State requirements for initial teacher certification vary; some require students to major in an academic discipline, while others allow an education major. Some states specify how many courses or hours students must complete in mathematics, science, and technology for elementary, middle school, and high school licensure, as well as for recertification. Middle or high school certification criteria may also include assessment of teachers' subject-matter knowledge. In some states, teachers may move through a number of levels of certification over the course of their careers. For example, teachers may receive "initial" certification upon entry into the profession, followed by a "professional" certificate after several years of refining their teaching skills and demonstrating proficiency in the classroom. The nonprofit National Board for Professional Teaching Standards (NBPTS) offers a relatively new form of certification (e.g., NBPTS, 2000a, 2000b), which allows experienced teachers to demonstrate and gain recognition for accomplished practice independent of any particular state's definitions of proficiency.

Interest in improving teaching quality has become more prominent at both state and national levels. Part of this attention is focused on teacher content knowledge, where there is concern, for example, that 30 percent of U.S. high school mathematics teachers overall, and a higher proportion of teachers in high-poverty schools, do not have a major or minor in their field (National Center for Educational Statistics [NCES] 1995, 1997b; Ingersoll, 1998).

Ongoing Professional Development

Professional learning opportunities present themselves to teachers in many ways and contexts (McLaughlin, 1993), forming what has been characterized by some as "a patchwork" rather than a coherent program of continuing education (Wilson and Berne, 1999, p. 174). Studies of professional development reveal discrepancies between what is known or believed about facilitating meaningful learning and what most mathematics, science, and technology teachers actually experience in these programs. Typically, teachers attend one-time events that deal with topics unrelated to any school priorities or issues regarding their teaching practice, and that provide little or no follow-up work to facilitate classroom implementation of any ideas learned (Garet et al., 1999; Shields et al., 1999).

The range of opportunities for teachers and other educators to engage in professional learning may be enhanced or constrained by the setting within which teachers work—that is, by the "infrastructure" of expertise and resources available to sustain such learning opportunities, and by incentives provided to encourage teachers to take advantage of those opportunities. Districts typically offer menus of professional development events and may organize other learning activities for teachers (Little, 1993), with the majority of formal learning opportunities (that is, those that "count" toward salary increments) organized and conducted outside the school. Professional associations and other groups specializing in professional development also offer a variety of experiences for teachers, including workshops, short courses, and network participation. Finally, teachers may complete courses offered through colleges and universities for personal and professional enrichment that may also contribute toward completing advanced degrees, meeting continuing certification requirements, or obtaining salary increases.

Informal learning opportunities for teachers may arise within their own schools, as they share ideas, struggle with problems of classroom practice, seek advice, and acquire new teaching insights. Teachers may also conduct action research projects, experiment with new materials or technologies, or visit other classrooms to work with or observe colleagues. In "professional development schools," novice teachers, faculty, and researchers from universities routinely collaborate with experienced teachers in ongoing activities to improve school teaching. School-based professional development may also be designed and facilitated by principals, curriculum coordinators, professional development specialists, or teacher leaders. These interventions are provided during planning periods or times that allow teachers to work with peers and facilitators. However, such practices are not the rule. In general, teachers of mathematics and science have relatively few regular times to plan, collaborate, or learn with their peers (Weiss et al., 1994; NRC, 1999a; NCES, 2000c).

Calls for improvements in professional development have increased dramatically over the last decade (Wilson and Berne, 1999; Loucks-Horsley and Matsumoto, 1999) and numerous publications have advanced principles or "beliefs" to guide the design of professional development (e.g., Little, 1993; Ball, 1996; Black and Atkin, 1996; Loucks-Horsley, Hewson, Love, and Stiles, 1998). The literature documents a growing consensus that professional development designs should incorporate teachers' prior experiences, active engagement, learning over time, close linkages to the school workplace, practicing and applying what is learned, and opportunities for follow-up with colleagues (Wilson and Berne, 1999); and there is an emerging consensus about the kinds of environments that facilitate teachers' learning (NRC, 1999c).

At the same time, Wilson and Berne (1999) point out that little is known about what teachers actually learn (or do not learn) from either traditional inservice work or more recent forms of professional development. While some studies show connections between professional development and increases in student learning (e.g., Cohen and Hill, 2000; Kennedy, 1998; Carpenter, Fennema, Peterson, Chiang, and Loef, 1989; Fennema, Franke, Carpenter, and Carey, 1993), much remains to be understood about the interrelationships among professional development, teacher learning, knowledge of subject matter, pedagogy, and student learning.

HOW STANDARDS MIGHT INFLUENCE TEACHER DEVELOPMENT

If nationally developed standards are influencing the preparation of new teachers, there would be increased alignment of policies and practice with the standards. States, districts, and postsecondary institutions would create systems that enable prospective teachers to gain the knowledge and skills needed to help students meet standards-based learning goals. In particular, analysis of teacher-preparation programs and course artifacts would verify that the professional development standards are being interpreted and implemented as intended. Evidence would also confirm that college and university educators are aligning the content and pedagogy of undergraduate courses, conventional teacher preparation programs, and alternate certification programs with expectations of the national standards. State licensure systems would set criteria for initial certification that require graduates to demonstrate their understanding of the standards, knowledge of the content and pedagogy described therein, and ability to implement standards-based instructional programs.

Policies and fiscal investments at local, state, and federal levels would focus on recertification criteria, professional development opportunities, and system-wide support strategies aligned with nationally developed standards in the three subject areas. Experienced teachers well-versed in the teaching, assessment, and professional development standards would be offered leadership roles to assist schools in implementing needed reforms.

States and localities would provide a rich "infrastructure" to support standards-based mathematics, science, and technology teaching. Administrators at school and district levels would possess the skills, commitment, and capabilities to promote collegial planning and dialogue about content, teaching, and assessment as called for in the national standards. Teachers would be motivated to enhance their understanding of standards-based content, ways to arrange appropriate learning experiences, and techniques for assessing what students understand. Recertification criteria and teacher evaluations would focus on evidence verifying the knowledge, skills, and practices advocated by the standards.

If standard-based visions of equity are being implemented, teacher preparation programs would prepare prospective teachers to teach in diverse classrooms, and teachers skilled in implementing standards-based education would be distributed so that all learners have access to high-quality learning opportunities.

THE TEACHER DEVELOPMENT CHANNEL AND NATIONALLY DEVELOPED STANDARDS

The Framework questions (see Figure 3-3) offer guidance in studying the influence of standards on teacher preparation, certification, and ongoing professional development by raising questions such as these:

- *How has the teacher development component of the education system responded to the introduction of nationally developed standards?*
- *How are the standards being received and interpreted by higher education institutions in redesigning their teacher preparation and inservice programs, by state agencies in determining criteria for teacher licensure, and by schools and districts in hiring teachers and providing for their inservice learning?*
- *What actions regarding allocations of time and resources have been taken by various components of the system to motivate and support needed professional development in relation to standards?*
- *To what extent have teachers acquired more substantive knowledge of standards-based content and improved skills regarding pedagogy and collegial activity, as called for in the standards?*
- *To what extent have teachers' classroom and professional practices changed in relation to the teaching and assessment standards?*
- *To what extent are all students provided with teachers who have the skills and content knowledge needed to teach the content described in the standards?*
- *In summary, who has been affected and in what ways?*

Studies that address such questions will enable the accumulation of evidence to formulate answers to the Framework's two overarching questions: *How has the system responded to the introduction of nationally developed standards?* and *What are the consequences for student learning?*

The next chapter explores the third main channel of potential influence of nationally developed standards within the U.S. education system—assessment and accountability. That channel, when combined with the two already considered—curriculum and teacher development—completes the Framework's mapping of key avenues of influence on policies, programs, and practices within the education system.

CHAPTER 6

ASSESSMENT AND ACCOUNTABILITY: WHAT KINDS OF ASSESSMENT ARE USED AND FOR WHAT PURPOSES?

Assessment, traditionally used by individual teachers to monitor student learning and to provide a basis for assigning grades, has always been a critical component of the education system (Glaser and Silver, 1994). Over the years, however, the character of educational assessment has changed. In the 1970s, concerns about reading and computational literacy led many states to implement minimum competency programs as a requirement for high school graduation. The role of assessment continued to evolve, as policy makers turned to assessment as a way to improve education. Standards-based reforms of the 1990s gave assessment increasing visibility, sending signals about the successes and failures of schools and school districts, as well as of individual students.

Assessments generate information and, depending on the nature and use of the information obtained, can play multiple roles in education. Accountability involves using some of this information to generate incentives to validate or change the behaviors of students and educators. Taken together, assessments and accountability policy constitute a third channel through which education reform ideas may flow. Various types of assessments—formative classroom assessment, classroom tests, state and local tests, college entrance and placement practices, tests for teacher certification—all interact with other elements in the education system, sometimes in unanticipated ways.

Considering the roles of assessment in K-12 educational practice includes study of four key elements:

- How accountability interacts with assessments
- How teachers conduct and use classroom assessment
- How states and districts use assessments for accountability
- How assessments influence postsecondary education

choices

ASSESSMENT AND ACCOUNTABILITY IN THE EDUCATION SYSTEM

Accountability

The pervasiveness, political importance, and potential influence of assessment on student learning make it a potent tool for change. Compared to other vehicles for change, such as long-term professional development, assessment is an attractive strategy to policy makers, since tests are relatively inexpensive to construct and administer. Moreover, assessment can be externally mandated and implemented rapidly, yielding visible results (Linn, 2000).

As the standards movement extended beyond standards designed by the educational community for use by educators to a vehicle for motivating school change, states began designing assessments to measure student learning against those standards. Other policies also contributed to the increased role of assessment. For example, Title I of Improving America's Schools Act of 1994 (PL 103-382 108) and the Individuals with Disabilities Education Act Amendments of 1997 (PL 105-17 111) require that states develop high-quality assessments to measure performance on high standards for all students, including those with disabilities. In addition, states participating in the second Education Summit in Palisades, New York, in March 1996 agreed to establish clear academic standards for student achievement in core subject areas and to assist schools in accurately measuring student progress toward reaching these standards (National Education Goals Panel, 1996).

Assessments provide a systematic way to inform students,

teachers, parents, policy makers, and the public about student performance. The reporting of test results represents the simplest form of accountability. Stronger incentives for educational change are provided by accountability mechanisms that use information from assessments to make consequential decisions about students, teachers, or schools. Assessment and accountability policies can provide clear direction for teachers and principals in terms of student outcomes and can become a positive impetus for instructional and curricular changes (Goertz, 2000; Kelley, Odden, Milanowski, and Heneman, 2000; O'Day and Smith, 1993; Popham, 2000). When assessments are aligned with learning goals, accountability systems can motivate classroom instruction to focus on those outcomes (Stecher, Barron, Kaganoff, and Goodwin, 1998). Thus, policy makers and educators in many states view assessment linked with accountability as a powerful strategy for ensuring that all students are held to the same set of high standards (Grissmer and Flanagan, 1998; Massell et al., 1997; Olson, 2001).

Assessments can drive change at different levels of the system, for example, by informing the public about the overall state of achievement or by informing those who make decisions about teacher certification, allocation of resources, or rewards and sanctions for schools. Tests based on large, statistically selected national samples, such as the National Assessment of Educational Progress (NAEP), are designed to provide a national overview of U.S. student achievement over time (National Research Council [NRC], 1999b), often spurring state and national efforts targeted at reform. Although NAEP results provide no information about individual students, many state assessments are designed to compare individual student performance levels to specific state standards.

Assessments are designed to serve particular purposes, and assessment experts warn that a test designed for one purpose is unlikely to be appropriate for an entirely different purpose. One major issue in the late 1990s concerned the inappropriate use of tests as evidence of the success or failure of schools and schooling (Linn and Herman, 1997; NRC, 1999b; American Educational Research Association, 2000).

Assessment and accountability practices apply to educators as well as to K-12 students. National concern about teacher quality (NRC, 2001b; Lewis et al., 1999; Education Trust, 1999a) has given rise to assessments for prospective and practicing teachers. These vary from tests such as the Praxis I and II, used by many colleges and universities as an entry or exit requirement for teacher education programs, to state tests that prospective teachers must pass before they receive licensure. Some states have instituted more complex processes for initial licensure, including evaluation of portfolios of student work and videos of classroom practice during induction years. Teachers seeking National Board for Professional Teaching Standards (NBPTS) certification must satisfactorily complete a series of assessments based on videos of their classroom teaching and analysis of student work, as well as tests of their content knowledge (NBPTS, 2001).

Classroom Assessment

Assessments designed or selected by teachers are critical components of education assessment. Teachers use assessment to inform instructional decisions, motivate and reward students, assign grades, and report student progress to families. They continuously assess what students know and how they have come to that understanding by, for example, reviewing homework, managing discussions, asking questions, listening to student conversations, answering questions, and observing student strategies as they work in class. Assessment and instruction interact when teachers collect evidence about student performance and use it to shape their teaching (NRC, 2001a; Shepard, 2000; Black and Wiliam, 1998; Niyogi, 1995).

Teachers also give students "summative" assessments regularly as end-of-unit and end-of-year tests. Teachers build their understanding of formal assessment from their own classroom experiences, interactions with colleagues, assessment materials accompanying textbooks, courses in preservice and professional development programs, and their familiarity with standardized assessments. They may adopt a variety of forms of assessment, from multiple-choice tests to writing assignments to performance-based assessments guided by scoring rubrics. Teachers may use student portfolios to document student learning over time, which, in the case of technology, may often take the form of student-created projects.

State and District Assessment and Accountability Policies

Nearly all states have adopted assessment programs, often as the centerpiece of their accountability strategies (*Education Week*, 2001; Council of Chief State School Officers [CCSSO], 1999b). From a policy viewpoint, state tests sometimes define the "content of most worth" for schools and their teachers. School districts may use their own or commercially developed tests to measure their progress against national norms, to evaluate their own programs, or to monitor the level of individual student learning for placement purposes.

Some state and local district assessments are "high stakes." That is, they carry important consequences for students, teachers, or schools, such as promotion to the next grade, salary allocations, or monetary bonuses for schools (CCSSO, 1999a). Some states also provide extra staff and resources to assist low-performing schools or districts; some give financial rewards for high levels of performance or for improvements in student outcomes.

States and districts may use "norm-referenced" tests, where a student's reported score is compared to the scores of other students in some reference population. Schools may use the results of those tests to "track" students into courses with different content and achievement expectations, a practice that has raised concerns about adversely affecting minorities and students in certain geographic areas (Oakes et al., 1990; Shepard, 1991; Glaser and Silver, 1994). Publishers of norm-referenced tests study state curricular guidelines and existing textbooks, and establish test specifications based on the content they identify. In some instances, publishers customize tests according to the criteria of a particular state or district. Generally, such tests are not released to educators or the public; their confidential nature often makes it difficult to analyze what the tests actually measure.

Over half of the states and some districts use some form of "criterion-referenced" assessments (CCSSO, 1998). Such assessments attempt to establish whether a student has met a particular performance level by estimating the extent to which each student has learned certain content, regardless of how others might have performed (NRC, 1999d). A number of states and districts have attempted to use portfolios to document student learning over time, but have encountered substantial problems due to scoring difficulties and costs (Koretz, 1998; Stecher, 1998).

In addition to state tests, school districts may use a variety of other tests, which interact with decisions made about curriculum and instruction. Tests that measure what students know overall are different from those designed to measure what students have learned within a particular course or time interval, placing different demands on what teachers are expected to teach. From test to test, the conditions and the nature of the content tested may vary widely. For example, one test may allow the use of calculators, another may not; one may emphasize mastery of science terms, another may emphasize understanding of science concepts. Some assessment reports may disaggregate the data, highlighting changes in performance for students of different ethnicities, socioeconomic backgrounds, or cultures, leading to greater focus on students within those groups.

College Entrance and Placement Practices

Within two years after high school graduation, nearly 75 percent of U.S. students will enroll in a postsecondary institution (Education Trust, 1999b; National Center for Education Statistics, 1997a). Consequently, college entrance and placement assessments guide many decisions made by high school students and teachers, as well as decisions about those students made by postsecondary institutions. The most important assessments for those students—customarily the SAT or ACT—affect college admission. Other assessments, including advanced placement tests and those administered by colleges and universities, guide course and program placement. For example, placement tests for introductory mathematics at the college level are used to identify students for remediation or acceleration and may as a result influence the content taught at the secondary level (Hebel, 2001).

Impact and Unintended Consequences of Assessment

The interpretation and consequent influence of assessment as a measure of educational improvement are matters of debate. On the one hand, such assessments can set levels of acceptable performance for all students and provide benchmarks against which teachers, students, and states can view their own educational accomplishments. The assessments may motivate educators to change their practices and decision makers to modify their policies. If politicians and educators believe that full alignment of content, instruction, and assessment will positively affect student outcomes, they may invest considerable effort in trying to ensure that such alignment is in place across all levels of the education system.

On the other hand, researchers and others have raised concerns about using large-scale assessments to monitor student and school performance (Resnick and Resnick, 1992). Large-scale assessments may not provide valid and comparable measures of performance for all students. States or districts may exclude some students from their assessment programs (generally second-language learners), or withhold student test results that are not valid measures of what students know or are not comparable to scores of students generated under regular testing conditions.

Questions often arise regarding scoring procedures and what it means to "pass" a particular test. For example, some researchers claim that the use of averages in reporting test scores—one of the most common strategies in assessment—is inappropriate, arguing that average scores fail to account for variability within the population (Meyer, 1996). There is evidence that the choice of controlling variables (e.g., socioeconomic status variables, prior achievement) and summary statistics (e.g., mean gain, mean difference) help determine what conclusions are drawn (Linn, 2000; Clotfeler and Ladd, 1996). Factors such as when a test is administered during the school year also affect conclusions about apparent growth in student achievement (Linn, 2000). In addition, there is concern about the validity of what assessment data seem to indicate about student performance. A recurring pattern is evident in the implementation of a new test—a decrease in student performance the first year, followed by sharp increases in achievement in subsequent years—that may overstate actual student growth (Linn, 2000).

Large-scale, high-stakes tests can produce unintended effects. When rewards and consequences are attached to test performance, high scores may become the classroom focus and may well change the nature of instruction (Haertel, 1999; Glaser and Silver, 1994; Linn and Herman, 1997). This in turn may generate inflated scores that are not representative of what students actually know (Koretz, Linn, Dunbar, and Shepard, 1991; Madaus, 1988; Stecher and Barron, 1999; Klein, Hamilton, McCoffey, and Stecher, 2000). A key objective in aligning content and assessment is to help shape instruction and to raise expectations for student performance. Questions arise, however, about whether teachers are focusing on teaching the underlying standards-based content or simply teaching to the test. Some argue that high-stakes tests tend to narrow the curriculum. That is, teachers reduce instructional time devoted to problem-solving and open-ended investigations, and restrict their expectations for student learning to the particular knowledge and skills included on the test (Dwyer, 1998; Barton, 1999). The use of assessments for purposes for which they were not designed may partially account for some of that concern, but similar effects have been linked to tests even when used as intended (Stecher and Barron, 1999).

Assessments do more than simply provide information about achievement, they also specify expectations for student knowledge and performance (NRC, 1993, 1996), providing "an operational definition of standards, in that they define in measurable terms what teachers should teach and students should learn" (NRC, 1996, pp. 5–6). The development and use of assessments keyed to the standards to support teaching, to drive educational improvement, and to support accountability are indicators of possible influences attributable to nationally developed standards.

HOW STANDARDS MIGHT INFLUENCE ASSESSMENT AND ACCOUNTABILITY

If nationally developed standards are influencing assessment policies and practices, assessments would be aligned with learning outcomes embodied in the standards. In particular, if state assessments and standards are aligned with the nationally developed standards, assessment at all levels would include problem solving and inquiry in addition to other skills and knowledge. Teachers would use classroom assessment results to inform instructional decisions and to provide feedback to students about their learning. Teachers, administrators, and policy makers would employ multiple sources of evidence regarding what a student knows and is able to do, as is called for in the standards, rather than relying on a single source.

Developers of student assessments would be familiar with nationally developed assessment and content standards and create assessment materials that reflect the standards by having appropriate items, clear examples of the kinds of performance that students are expected to demonstrate, criteria by which these performances are evaluated, and reports that inform instruction as well as measure achievement. Assessment results would be reported in language accessible to parents and other stakeholders, helping them to understand what the tests measure and how results labeled as "proficient" or "basic" should be interpreted.

States and districts would have a comprehensive plan for administering the array of assessments they use with students, and the plan would enable teachers to pursue the vision of the standards as well as prepare students to take those assessments that are high stakes. Incentives linked to accountability would encourage standards-based reforms, with policies in place to ensure that schools and teachers have standards-based professional development opportunities, instructional materials, and appropriate resources to enhance their efforts to raise performance levels of their students. Finally, college entrance and placement tests would measure content that is valued by standards created at the national level and contain tasks aligned with those standards.

THE ASSESSMENT AND ACCOUNTABILITY CHANNEL AND NATIONALLY DEVELOPED STANDARDS

The Framework questions (see Figure 3-3) can guide the study of possible influences of standards on K-12 assessment practices and policies. Useful questions focused on this channel of influence include:

- *How has the assessment and accountability component of the education system responded to the introduction of nationally developed standards?*
- *To what extent have teachers modified their assessment practices in line with the recommendations of the standards?*
- *Are teachers using classroom assessment to monitor student progress in relation to the standards and adjust their instruction accordingly?*

- *To what extent are state and district assessment and accountability systems aligned with the content, instruction, and assessment called for in the standards?*
- *What changes have states and school districts made in the use of assessments and in the infrastructure to support the implementation of standards-based assessment programs?*
- *To what extent do assessment systems report student achievement for demographic subgroups of the population so policy makers can determine whether all students are making progress towards higher standards?*
- *What actions have been taken to align college entrance and placement tests with nationally developed standards?*

Studies that explore answers to such questions will inform the two overarching questions: *How has the system responded to the introduction of nationally developed mathematics, science, and technology standards?* and *What are the consequences for student learning?*

The next chapter deals with influences external to the education system that might also have an impact on how standards affect classroom teaching and learning. As the chapter points out, those influences may arise within public, professional, and political communities.

CHAPTER 7

CONTEXTUAL FORCES THAT INFLUENCE THE EDUCATION SYSTEM

In addition to affecting aspects of the education system, standards may also interact with various sectors of society and the general public in numerous ways. This chapter explores the public and political arenas within which the U.S. education system operates. Fullan (2000) uses the term "outside forces" to characterize those external factors and their possible pressures on the education system. He notes that in this era of education reform "outside forces" tend to move "inside" accompanied, for example, by demands for better educational performance and greater accountability. This chapter explores ways that key outside forces can interact with components of the education system—and with nationally developed standards.

WHO AFFECTS THE EDUCATION SYSTEM FROM "OUTSIDE"?

Publicly supported education is a mainstay of U.S. democracy. The public's high interest in and concern about education are well documented in public opinion polls and by the prominence of education issues in political campaigns (Rose and Gallup, 2000; Johnson and Aulicino, 1998; Robelen, 2000; Sack and Jacobson, 2000; Keller, 2000). Overall public support for "high academic standards" in public schools has remained strong since national educational goals were established in 1989 by President George H.W. Bush and the nation's governors (Public Agenda, 2000; Johnson and Aulicino, 1998). One study within nine states and twenty-five local school districts showed that public and political support for higher standards were bipartisan and sustained—although the support was relatively superficial (Massell et al., 1997).

Decision making within the education system is, in large part, a political process, involving a number of key players. Kirst, Anhalt, and Marine (1997) note the importance of legislators in decision-making regarding curriculum; Tyack and Cuban (1995) note that "powerful sponsors adept at persuading local school boards, state legislatures, state departments of education, and accrediting agencies" are central in institutionalizing reforms. And, since the 1980s, governors have acquired increasing authority and influence regarding governance of state-level education systems (Fuhrman and Elmore, 1994; Stricherz, 2001).

Elected leaders and other governmental officials make decisions within the context of the political realities in which they operate. Candidates campaign on education platforms they believe will gain voter approval, and newcomers may be elected by constituents dissatisfied with decisions of previous office holders. For example, in 2000, the electorate voted new members to the Kansas School Board who were committed to including biological evolution in the state curriculum framework and state assessments, in sharp contrast to the state's preceding Board, which had restricted the teaching of this topic (Belluck, 2000). Sometimes public officials use their position to influence others and advance particular reforms, as Governor Hunt did in persuading the North Carolina legislature to establish incentives and rewards for teachers seeking NBPTS certification (North Carolina Public Schools, 2000). Elected officials also listen to constituents, as a Congressional subcommittee did in hearing testimony from mathematics professor David Klein, who objected to the process used by the U.S. Department of Education to identify "exemplary mathematics curricula" based on their extent of alignment with nationally developed standards (Klein, 2000).

Outside Forces Affecting Decision Making

Education-related decisions by officials at all levels of government may be influenced by varied concerns. The U.S. recession of the early 1980s and pressures created by global competitiveness heightened the public's economic concerns, and in particular, those of business leaders. Some influential leaders who view education as the key to a stronger economic future have promoted new accountability initiatives and provided incentives to stimulate improvements in schools.

Similarly, corporations and their representatives have become involved in influencing education policy at local, state, and federal levels, in their pursuit of employees who possess the skills and knowledge needed by a productive workforce. Individually and through organizations such as the Business Roundtable, businesses offer advice to elected officials regarding educational policies.

Educational concerns may motivate professional organizations, parents, and others to work toward particular goals. For example, education and professional associations and their government relations representatives lobby federal and state lawmakers regarding policy decisions, including financial allocations. Teachers and administrators may use information from national associations to encourage local school officials to limit the sizes of classes assigned to laboratory rooms, select particular textbooks or curricular programs, or increase funding for instructional technology. Parents concerned that their children's educational interests are not well served by high-stakes assessments may speak out in opposition to state-level testing or even keep their children at home on state-testing days.

In particular, concerns regarding equity, stemming from efforts of organized groups, federal legislation, and court orders, may affect decisions about resource allocations, testing accommodations, and curricular offerings. At local levels, parents and guardians may work to ensure their children's access to high-level mathematics courses, well-prepared technology teachers, and culturally appropriate science programs. Civil rights groups may lobby state legislators for changes in education funding to ensure that all children have access to high-quality teachers and learning opportunities.

Education-related decisions of officeholders and other policy makers are also influenced by media that convey information and shape public perceptions. Widespread U.S. media coverage of Third International Mathematics and Science Study findings alerted the public and politicians to the fact that U.S. student test score results often compared unfavorably to those of nations regarded as economic competitors. Those messages played a role in spurring new actions intended to improve U.S. mathematics and science education, such as the work of the National Commission on Mathematics and Science Teaching for the 21st Century (2000). At the local level, news stories and editorials centering on the lack of textbooks and laboratory facilities in urban schools may heighten public awareness of inequities in the U.S. education system. Local media coverage of students' achievement scores also informs and influences community views.

Outside Forces Affecting Components Within the Education System

In addition to exerting influence through the political system, some businesses, education and professional organizations, and others have acted to influence the education system directly. Major chemical, pharmaceutical, technology, and aerospace firms have invested in science education reform for many years—for example, some corporate officials work with educators to help school districts develop and implement local strategic plans to provide inquiry-centered science programs for all students (National Science Resources Center, 1999). Organizations supported by corporations have also intervened directly. For example, the National Action Council for Minorities in Engineering, Inc. has worked to attract minorities to engineering and supported them in their schooling. National associations of science, mathematics, and technology educators, such as the National Council of Teachers of Mathematics, the National Science Teachers Association, the International Technology Education Association, and their chapters and affiliates, contribute to the ongoing professional development of their members by producing a wide range of periodicals and other publications; holding conventions and workshops at national, regional, and local levels; and organizing other programs. Some informal educational institutions, such as science centers and museums, and some professional societies, such as the American Chemical Society, also create and publish curriculum materials and provide elementary and secondary teachers with professional development opportunities.

HOW CAN NATIONALLY DEVELOPED STANDARDS INFLUENCE THOSE "OUTSIDE" THE SYSTEM? HOW MIGHT THEY, IN TURN, INFLUENCE THE EDUCATION SYSTEM?

Standards are more likely to have an influence on the education system if they are supported by the "outside" forces, rather than being ignored or even opposed. If the standards are influencing individuals and groups external to the education system as intended, decisions enacted by elected officials and policy makers would show support for standards-based reforms. Professional associations in the forefront of the development of national standards for mathematics, science, and technology would lead national and local efforts to implement the standards, as well as work with elected officials and leaders to build a consensus in support of institutionalizing standards-based reforms.

The traditional school priorities of reading, writing, and arithmetic would be joined by science, technology, and a broader view of mathematics as new "basics" for all students. State and local school boards, reflecting and responding to constituents' views, would ensure that schools have adequate funding to provide students with learning experiences that will enable them to meet the nationally developed standards.

Professional associations would join together and collaborate with decision makers in establishing assessment and accountability programs that draw on multiple measures and address the full range of standards-based content and skills. The public would be informed of standards-based progress and supportive of continuing efforts. Attempts to weaken or dismantle standards-based education—whether to de-emphasize the place of mathematics, science, or technology in the curriculum; to limit assessment solely to skill development; or to reduce funding for professional development focused on standards-based instruction—would be met with vocal public criticism and opposed by policy makers.

On the other hand, standards may generate resistance and opposition by individuals and groups outside the system. In that case, scientists, mathematicians, engineers, and technology design professionals who disagree with the standards' vision of mathematics, science, and technology education, would argue, for example, that standards exclude important content or lack rigor. Such groups would work to influence views of policy makers or the public at large, affecting decisions and actions within the education system.

Opponents would encourage funding or programmatic decisions regarding curriculum, professional development, and accountability practices that inhibit implementation of the nationally developed standards, working to convince legislators, governors, and school boards that the fiscal, resource, or political costs associated with changes urged by the standards are inappropriate.

CONTEXTUAL FORCES AND NATIONALLY DEVELOPED STANDARDS

The Framework questions (see Figure 3-3) offer guidance in studying possible influences of standards on public and political forces outside the education system and the effect of those forces on the education system's channels of influence by raising questions such as these:

- *How have politicians, policy makers, the electorate, parents, business and industry, education organizations, and others responded to the introduction of nationally developed standards?*
- *How are the standards being received and interpreted by those outside forces?*
- *In response, what actions have politicians and the public taken regarding policies and funding in support of, or in opposition to, standards-based curricula, teacher development, and assessment and accountability systems?*
- *What changes, if any, have occurred in the opinions, activities, and decisions of governmental leaders and various public groups regarding mathematics, science, and technology education?*
- *What has been the resulting impact on the adoption of standards-based policies, programs, and practices in schools and districts?*
- *Who has been affected and how?*

Studies that address such questions will enable educators and policy makers to begin accumulating evidence and formulating answers to the Framework's two overarching questions: *How has the system responded to the introduction of nationally developed standards?* and *What are the consequences for student learning?*

The next—and final—chapter reviews the Framework in light of the channels and forces interacting within the education system, suggests a range of research-based uses for the Framework, and offers final comments from the Committee to those who use the Framework to consider the educational impact of nationally developed standards.

CHAPTER 8

USING THE FRAMEWORK

What does it mean to make use of the Framework in investigating possible influences of nationally developed standards on mathematics, science, and technology education? In addressing that question, this chapter first recaps the argument for the Framework; then describes and illustrates ways of using the Framework; and, finally, presents the Committee's aspirations for its use of such a framework.

Although this chapter outlines *possible* uses of the Framework, the Committee stops short of presenting a research agenda, which was not part of the Committee's charge. In illustrating how the Framework can be applied, the chapter considers what will be involved in seeking sound, useful answers to this document's overarching questions about the influence of nationally developed standards on programs, policies, practices, and student learning.

At this stage in the life cycle of national standards—more so for mathematics and science than technology—educators and policy makers would benefit from concerted efforts to address the two core questions: *How has the system responded to the introduction of nationally developed standards?* and *What are the consequences for student learning?*

THE FRAMEWORK IN REVIEW

This document's central argument began with the premise that to answer questions about the effects of nationally developed standards on the education system and student learning, a Framework is needed to represent the education system, how reform ideas (such as standards) move through the system, and possible system and learner responses to the standards. In essence, such a "framework" represents a conceptual map—a set of organizing categories and presumed relationships among them—and a set of guiding questions to prompt inquiry within the map's territory. Schematically, this document's Framework can be represented as in Figure 8-1.

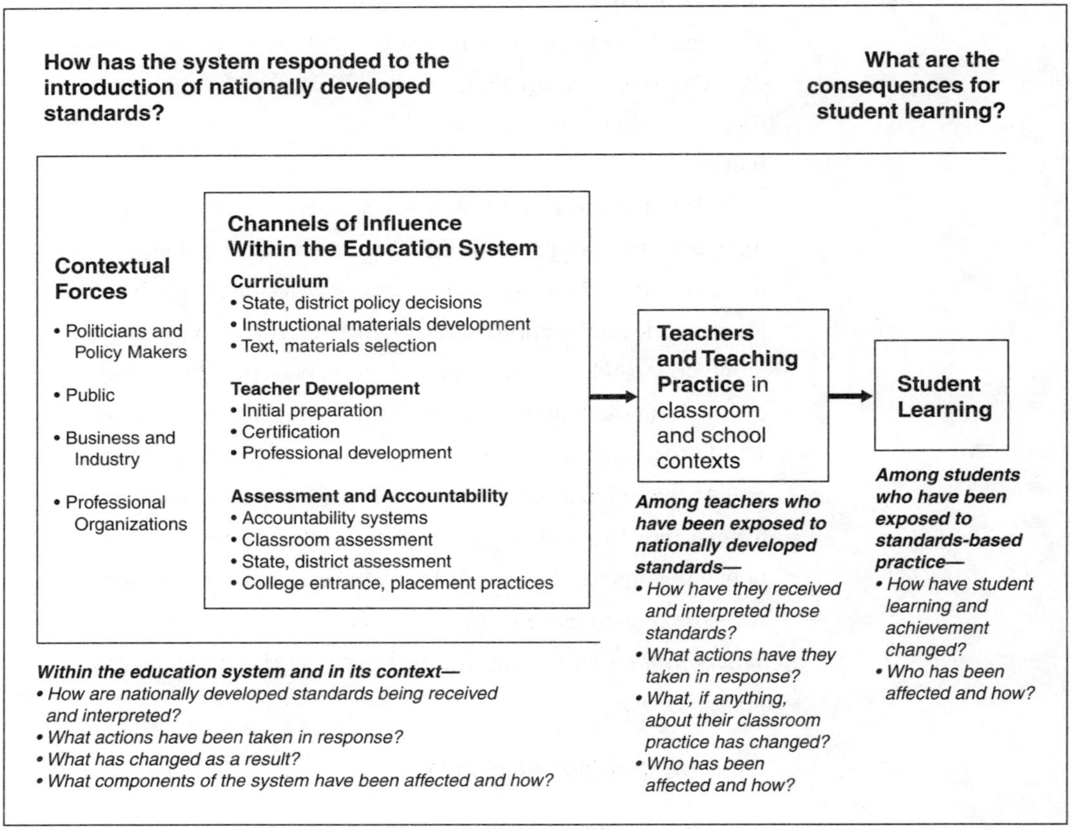

FIGURE 8-1 A Framework for Investigating the Influence of Nationally Developed Standards for Mathematics, Science, and Technology Education
NOTE: A full-sized copy of this Framework appears as Appendix B.

The logic implicit in the Framework can be summarized through a group of interrelated propositions:

1. *Nationally developed standards in mathematics, science, and technology represent a set of fundamental changes in the way these subjects have traditionally been taught, placing new demands on teachers and students.* The changes needed to move from established modes of teaching and learning to those advocated by the standards imply considerable new learning for both teachers and students. Standards-based practice presumes that teachers understand and have internalized much of what is asserted by national standards documents (e.g., that a core set of important ideas and skills in each content area can be identified and that all students can master those fundamental expectations).

2. *The expected influence of nationally developed standards on teaching practice and student learning is likely to be (a) indirect, taking place through proximate effects on other parts of the education system; (b) entangled (and sometimes confused) with other influential forces and conditions, such as broader state standards-based reforms; and (c) slowly realized and long term.* In other words, within the nation's decentralized system of education, notions of teaching and learning embedded in nationally developed standards do not have immediate pathways into classrooms. Rather, as these ideas move through channels that cross multiple levels of governance, various forces can alter how the standards are understood and acted upon. State-level standards-based reform movements, for example, have introduced numerous interpretations of "standards" and "assessments," some of which may not be in accord with ideas conveyed in the National Research Council (NRC), the National Council of Teachers of Mathematics (NCTM), and the International Technology Education Standards (ITEA) standards documents. Given the amount of new learning implied and the complexity of the education system, it would take a long time, if ever, before the visions conveyed by national standards documents would be fully realized. Also,

because national standards in the three subject areas have had different timelines, varying degrees and types of influence across subject areas are to be expected at any one time.

3. *Three core channels exist within the education system through which nationally developed standards can influence teaching and learning*. These channels of influence are (a) curriculum; (b) teacher development; and (c) assessment and accountability.

4. *The channels of influence are complex and interactive, and differ across subject-matter communities.* In other words, the channels operate differently within mathematics, science, and technology, creating different opportunities for—or barriers to—influence by the standards. Jointly or separately, the channels may alter the way standards are understood and realized. Public, political, and professional reactions can also affect these channels and shape the way standards reach and influence teaching and learning.

5. *Variability within the education system implies that students and teachers are likely to experience different influences, depending on locality, resources, participant background, and other factors.* Consequently, educational effects of national standards are unlikely to be monolithic. Instead, there may be effects that are constructive and others that are counterproductive, some weak, and others strong.

6. *The task for research—and hence for this Framework—is to help identify and document significant standards-based effects, as well as overall trends and patterns among those effects.* That is, the task is to provide evidence-based descriptions of the channels and mechanisms through which those effects take place and determine what conditions may be associated with particular effects.

7. *The ultimate focus is on the changes in students' knowledge and abilities that have occurred since standards have entered the system and that can be reasonably attributed to the influence of the standards. As part of this, it is essential to consider how standards have affected the achievement of all students, including those who were previously underrepresented in mathematics, science, and technology.*

8. *Eventually, nationally developed standards will be judged*

effective if resources, requirements, and practices throughout the system align with the standards and if students in standards-based classrooms demonstrate high achievement in knowledge and skills deemed important. Although there may be other grounds upon which individuals or groups elect to accept or reject the standards, the only empirical approach for making that judgment presumes that standards have had opportunities to permeate the education system, and, having done so, are associated with student-learning outcomes that can be judged as desirable or undesirable.

HOW THE FRAMEWORK CAN BE USED

The Framework is intended to help guide the sponsorship, design, and interpretation of research on nationally developed standards. The challenge is far from simple. The Framework lays out a complex domain of interacting forces and conditions that affect teaching and learning, any number of which can be touched by the influence of standards. Thus, no single study can investigate all the ways that national standards are, or could be, part of the education reform story. Rather, various types of studies, each guided by its own appropriate methodologies, will be needed to establish the scale and scope of influences, identify routes by which standards actually exert influence, and ascertain the direction and educational consequences of those influences.

Table 8-1 contains several hypothetical examples that illustrate how different macro and micro studies can "cover" the terrain of the Framework, and respond to one or more questions posed earlier in this document. Each of those hypothetical studies addresses only part of the broad territory embraced by the Framework. Multiple studies could collectively paint a more satisfactory picture of the effects of nationally developed standards if they were designed to generate complementary databases and were carefully synthesized.

In carrying out such research, the Framework offers assistance in several important ways: (1) situating existing studies within the

TABLE 8-1 Hypothetical Studies That Address One or More of the Framework Questions

	How are the nationally developed standards being received and interpreted?	What actions have been taken in response to the nationally developed standards?	What has changed as a result of nationally developed standards?	Who has been affected and how?
Analysis of media coverage of mathematics education can determine how often national standards are mentioned, which components of the standards are highlighted, how they are interpreted, and what value is attached to each.	●			
Expert reviews of documents can identify ways that state standards, assessments, and accountability systems may and may not reflect the content advocated in the national standards.	●			
National teacher surveys can reveal how aware teachers are of national standards, whether—and in what ways—they believe they are orienting their professional practices to these standards, and in what ways they are supported in their efforts to realize the standards.	●	●	●	

Comparative studies of reform-based curricula at a particular grade level can build understanding about how curriculum developers interpret the standards and how those interpretations may affect what students have opportunities to learn.	●	●		
Observational studies can reveal whether—and how—technology standards are realized in classroom practice within particular kinds of school settings.		●	●	
Case studies of district reform can explore the alignment of science curriculum and assessment policies with national standards and the nature and extent of district support teachers receive for teaching in standards-aligned ways.		●		
Quasi-experimental design studies can compare teachers' responses to standards and their students' performance in settings with differing degrees of exposure to, and support for, standards-based practices.			●	●
Case studies of standards-based classrooms can explore whether teachers adjust instruction appropriately, with respect for students' cultural backgrounds as well as ways of learning.			●	●

educational terrain relevant to the standards; (2) providing a conceptual tool for analyzing claims and inferences made by these studies; and (3) generating questions and hypotheses to be explored by future studies.

Situating Current Studies

The Framework can assist researchers in locating their work within a particular frame of reference and may highlight possible connections or lack of connections to other parts of the education system. Sponsors, investigators, and consumers of research findings should keep in mind aspects of the education territory that may and may not be addressed by particular studies or programs of investigation. Consider this study of standards implementation in a large urban district:

Standards, Assessments, and What Else? The Essential Elements of Standards-Based School Improvement (Briars and Resnick, 2000). The Pittsburgh Public Schools developed a core curriculum framework based on the NCTM Standards, adopted a standards-based assessment system (New Standards Mathematics Reference Examination) to be used in conjunction with the Iowa Test of Basic Skills, and adopted the National Science Foundation (NSF)-funded *Everyday Mathematics* program for grades K-5. An NSF Local Systemic Change grant provided funding for extensive professional development to prepare teachers to teach that curriculum. A study was conducted to evaluate the effects of this "nearly complete standards-based system" in mathematics, looking at student achievement on both the standards-based and traditional assessments. Recognizing that teachers varied in the extent to which they were implementing the curriculum as intended by the developers, the researchers also compared the performance of students in strong and weak implementing classrooms, disaggregating the data to see if differential results were obtained for groups defined by race/ethnicity.

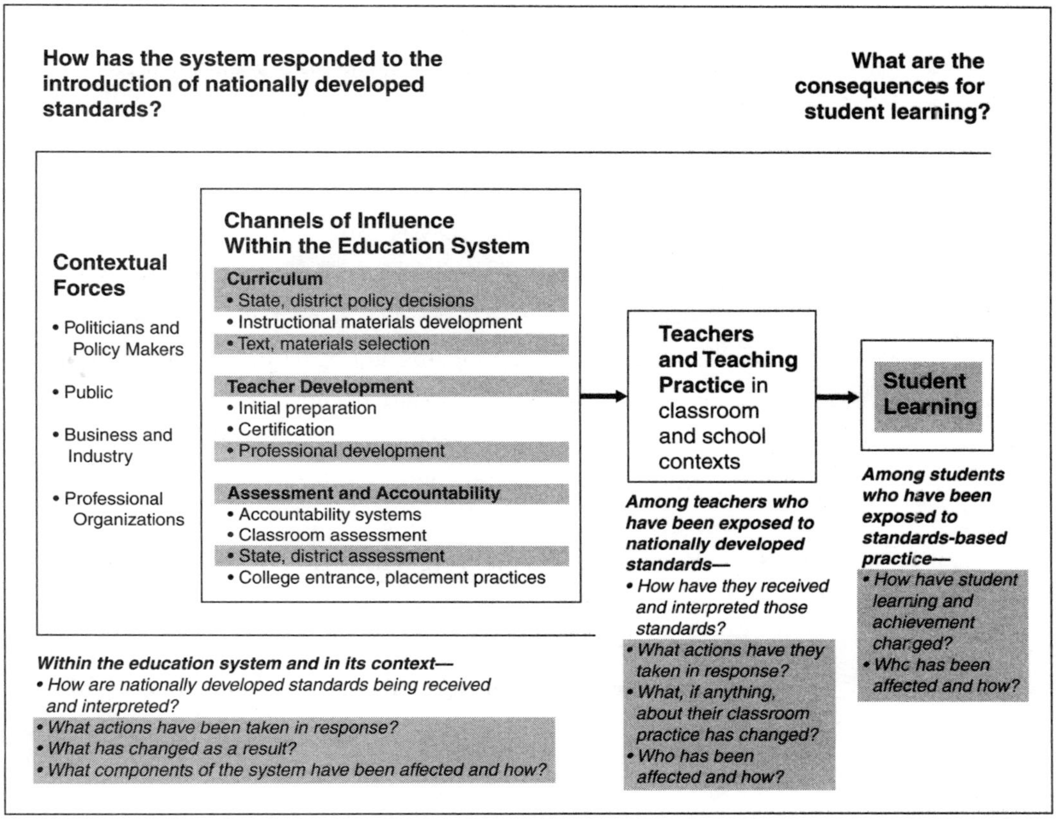

FIGURE 8-2 Parts of the Framework Addressed in the Briars and Resnick Study

This descriptive study can be mapped onto the Framework as shown in Figure 8-2. The shaded areas identify aspects of the Framework and related questions that are addressed in this analysis.

Studies with different purposes, designs, and evidence bases would cover different parts of the Framework. Consider this analysis:

Mathematics and Science Content Standards and Curriculum Frameworks (Council of Chief State School Officers, 1997). An expert panel reviewed state frameworks, standards documents, and related materials developed or revised during the period 1994 to

1997. The analysis sought to determine the extent that state curriculum frameworks, standards, and other materials were consistent with NCTM *Curriculum and Evaluation Standards for School Mathematics*, NRC *National Science Education Standards*, and American Association for the Advancement of Science *Benchmarks for Scientific Literacy*. The analysis also considered differences in content found in state mathematics and science frameworks or standards documents and main ideas and categories found in corresponding national standards, noting omissions and additions. The analysis pointed out how state documents acted as a "bridge" between nationally developed standards and local efforts to improve teaching and learning in these subject areas.

In contrast to the more broad-based Briars and Resnick study, this investigation focused in depth on one Framework component: State Policy Decisions within the Curriculum channel. Thus, shading would highlight only that particular feature of the Framework.

Examining Claims and Inferences Reported in Current Studies

In addition to helping locate relevant areas of research, the Framework offers a conceptual tool for assessing claims made by researchers. By highlighting multiple influences on teaching and learning, the Framework can suggest plausible alternative explanations for research findings. Referring to the Framework, scholars and other consumers of research can decide whether investigators accounted for all the plausible channels of influence on teaching and learning within the settings under study.

Without reference to a conceptual map such as the Framework, weak inferences may arise about the influence of standards. Ultimately, strong claims about positive or negative effects of nationally developed standards depend on a chain of evidence and inference linking promulgation of standards (at the national level) to particular sites (in schools and classrooms) within which standards-based ideas may be found to exert influence. As noted earlier, developing such a chain of evidence and inference will usually require multiple, coordinated studies.

An important caution: The Framework provides only a *conceptual* scheme for considering research claims, not *all* the information needed to assess research-based claims fully. A full analysis must include a host of "technical" considerations, such as standards of evidence, quality of measurement, and appropriateness of the research design. All of these concerns must be addressed in deciding whether particular research conclusions are trustworthy and rigorous.

Assuming comparable technical quality, several hypothetical examples illustrate how the Framework can help determine the soundness of research-based inferences.

- *A study of standards-based classroom practice in mathematics.* Imagine an investigation of standards-based mathematics teaching practice in a high socioeconomic environment that supports this kind of instruction, using a curriculum that embodies the principles of the NCTM standards. Assume that teachers have been well trained in this form of teaching and are committed to it. If, after sufficient time passes for the curriculum to have affected student learning across grades, a well-designed study documents indifferent or poor student results on assessments keyed to NCTM standards, it would be reasonable to infer that national mathematics standards contributed little to student learning—or might even have detracted from it. That inference could be further substantiated if other school settings less committed to NCTM standards produced more favorable results with comparable students.
- *A study of district investment in teacher professional development aligned with nationally developed content standards for technological literacy.* In a group of districts heavily emphasizing the principles and themes of ITEA content standards in their professional development and support programs, assessments of teacher knowledge

and pedagogical approaches might show that they have acquired the intended knowledge and skills, and that the teachers are attempting to realize these ideas in their teaching. Assuming a well-designed investigation into teachers' participation in standards-oriented professional development and the outcomes of that participation (including direct observations in their classrooms), it would be reasonable to infer that ITEA content standards had contributed to changes in those teachers' thinking and practice. (Establishing this particular claim does not necessarily imply that students learned more; that inference would require a different study, or an additional component to this investigation.) Once again, comparisons with other school sites less invested in standards-related content would help to establish the claim.

Note that the Framework helps to establish the conceptual soundness of research inferences by highlighting elements of the domain that, through a reasonable chain of evidence and inference, link national standards to classroom outcomes.

By contrast, the following hypothetical examples involve unwarranted conceptual leaps in their reported conclusions:

- *Analysis of student achievement gains in states that align their mathematics standards with NCTM standards.* Impressive student achievement gains in states that apparently embrace national mathematics standards invite the possible conclusion that the standards contributed to the improvements in student performance. But even assuming a technically sound analysis of test score trends that took into account known correlates of student achievement scores (e.g., student socioeconomic status), the inference is weak at best, or even fallacious, if the analysis did not consider other components highlighted by the Framework. Those conditions include alignment of the mathematics achievement measures with the standards, local interpretation of state and national curricular guidance, and the extent of standards-based classroom practice. In the absence of those considerations, there are too many other plausible explanations for the achievement gains to place any confidence in the inference that national standards had anything to do with them.

- *An investigation of declining science scores in a district committed to NRC standards.* Declines in student performance on district science assessments within a setting that has tried to encourage standards-related instruction may suggest to observers that the national standards are detrimental to student learning. Even if the investigation were carefully designed and executed, it would not support that conclusion, unless relevant components highlighted by the Framework were taken into account: alignment between the district's science assessments and the curriculum, teachers' interpretations of the standards and attempts to realize them in classroom instruction, and the extent of professional development for teachers unfamiliar with standards-based classroom practice.

In short, consumers of research, with the Framework in hand, can examine the results and conclusions of studies—or sets of studies—guided by questions such as these:

Does the study . . .

- *establish a plausible, evidence-based chain of influence that connects nationally developed standards to particular elements of the system under investigation?* The Framework highlights components that might be part of that chain of influence.
- *address plausible alternative explanations that could be advanced to account for observed effects or outcomes?* The Framework highlights alternative forces and conditions that may influence effects or outcomes.
- *consider interactions among different channels of influence that can convey either mutually reinforcing or contradictory messages to teachers and schools about standards-based practices?* The Framework lays out

the three primary channels of influence by which national standards could affect teaching and learning and notes ways these can interact with one another.

- *allow sufficient time for the education components under investigation to have been affected by nationally developed standards?* The Framework demonstrates the complexity of the system through which messages about standards-based practice must move, thus the effects may become visible only after an extended period of time.

Again, these are not all of the important questions to be asked about the findings and conclusions of research related to nationally developed standards in mathematics, science, or technology education. Other important questions include congruence of the research design with the research questions, execution of the design, adequacy of the database, and quality of data-analysis approaches. Still, the Framework establishes a conceptual map that provides relevance and meaning for answers to such additional questions.

Generating Questions and Hypotheses for Future Investigations

The Framework can help pinpoint areas of potential influences operating within the education system that may or may not have been considered by particular studies. This third main application of the Framework has two parts:

- *Assembling knowledge.* The Framework offers a basis for assembling knowledge gained from existing studies. Using Framework components as organizers, research syntheses and reviews can summarize what has been learned about the extent to which the education system has changed in response to nationally developed standards, particularly in terms of classroom practice and student learning.

- *Identifying gaps.* Gaps in current research can be identified by considering questions that could be (but have not been) asked about elements and relationships within the Framework. By highlighting where research attention has been most and least focused, the Framework can help researchers—and sponsors of research—target issues and areas of concern that merit more study.

As noted earlier, relatively few studies have investigated the relationships among professional development, teacher knowledge, instructional practice, and student achievement, either generally or with regard to national standards (Kennedy, 1998; Wilson and Berne, 1999). This paucity of studies regarding potentially important avenues for standards to reach classroom practice and student learning may signal a need to fill the gap.

Even, in areas where substantial numbers of studies have been completed, the Framework can highlight additional questions not yet extensively posed or answered. For example, a nagging concern within the broader standards-based reform movement regarding the equitable distribution of standards-based practice and equitable accountability systems (McKeon, Dianda, and McLaren, 2001) suggests an aspect of the story about the influence of national standards that may deserve greater attention. The relevant question in the Framework—*Who is affected and how?*—encourages researchers to explore possible differential effects of standards within diverse student populations and settings, while taking into account the varied capacities of teachers, schools, and districts to engage in standards-based practice.

Other examples can be readily envisioned. One important advance in cumulative understanding of nationally developed standards in mathematics, science, and technology education would be to assemble and map current knowledge using the Framework so that gaps and opportunities for further study emerge.

ASPIRATIONS FOR FRAMEWORK-DRIVEN RESEARCH ON NATIONALLY DEVELOPED STANDARDS

The Framework is offered in the hope that it will be useful to producers, consumers, and sponsors of research regarding central questions about the influence of nationally developed standards on mathematics, science, and technology education. Applications of the Framework described earlier will help to inform opinions and debate about those standards.

Three major aspirations of the Committee regarding use of the Framework are highlighted below.

1. *The Framework should be regarded as an evolving conceptual picture, rather than a definitive final statement.* In that spirit, the Framework should continue to evolve, informed by accumulating knowledge about standards-based reforms. It is essential that researchers build their understanding of the influence of nationally developed standards in terms of *some* overarching model of the education system (or subsystem) within which standards play out. The schematic of the Framework presented in this document can be regarded as one sketch of such a system, including the dynamics of influence contained within it.

2. *The Framework should stimulate different forms of inquiry into influences of nationally developed standards.* Given the complex and interactive nature of the territory within which standards have been enacted, a mosaic of evidence from many different types of studies is more likely to build overall understanding of the influence of standards than the results of a few purportedly comprehensive studies.

3. *The Framework should help guard against the superficiality that often permeates debate about high-visibility national policies by stimulating a critical view of claims regarding either the success or the failure of the standards.* Strong conclusions about effects or implications of nationally developed standards presume an understanding of the entire education system (encompassed by the Framework) and

presentation of a chain of evidence that connects the emergence of particular education practices, policies, or learning outcomes to the influence of standards.

All U.S. youth deserve access to the best possible education in mathematics, science, and technology. In pursuit of that goal, the education community should complete a comprehensive, critical appraisal of the power and limits of nationally developed standards. That appraisal is still far from being realized. Public conversations about the worth and impact of standards in mathematics, science, and technology—or about standards-based reforms in general—will continue. The Framework offered here is intended to help the education research community contribute to that debate with reasoned voices based on evidence and sound inference.

REFERENCES

American Association for the Advancement of Science. (1989). *Science for all Americans: A Project 2061 report on literacy goals in science, mathematics, and technology*. Washington, DC: Author.

American Association for the Advancement of Science. (1993). *Benchmarks for science literacy*. New York: Oxford University Press.

American Association for the Advancement of Science. (2000). *Middle grades mathematics textbooks: A benchmarks-based evaluation*. Washington, DC: Author.

American Educational Research Association. (2000). Position statement of the American Educational Research Association concerning high-stakes testing in preK-12 education. *Educational Researcher, 29*(8), 24-25.

Anderson, R.D. (1996). Final Technical Research Report: *Study of curriculum reform: Findings and conclusions, Volume 1*. Research conducted under contract No. RR91172001 with OERI. Washington, DC: U.S. Government Printing Office.

Anderson, R.D., and Helms, J.V. (2001). The Ideal of Standards and The Reality of Schools: Needed Research. *Journal of Research in Science Teaching, 38*(1), 3-16.

Anderson, R.D., and Mitchener, C.P. (1994). Research on Science Teacher Education. In D.L. Gabel (Ed.), *Handbook of Research on Science Teaching and Learning*. New York: Macmillan.

Armstrong, J., Davis, A., Odden, A., and Gallagher, J. (1998). *The impact of state policies on improving science curriculum*. Denver, CO: Education Commission of the States.

Ball, D.L. (1996). Teacher learning and the mathematics reforms: What do we think we know and what do we need to learn? *Phi Delta Kappan*, 77, 500-508.

Barton, P.E. (1999). *Too much testing of the wrong kind; too little of the right kind in K-12 education*. Princeton, NJ: Educational Testing Service.

Battista, M.T. (1999). The Mathematical Miseducation of America's Youth: Ignoring Research and Scientific Study in Education. *Phi Delta Kappan, 80*(6), 424-433.

Becker, J.P. and Jacob B. (2000). The Politics of California School Mathematics: The Anti-Reform of 1997-99. *Phi Delta Kappan, 81*(7), 529-537.

Belluck, P. (2000, August 3). Evolution's Foes Dealt a Defeat in Kansas Vote. *The New York Times*. Available: http://college2.nytimes.com/guests/articles/2000/08/03/592031.xml. [Accessed August 30, 2001.]

Black, P., and Wiliam, D. (1998). Inside the Black Box: Raising Standards Through Classroom Assessment. *Phi Delta Kappan, 80*(2), 139-144.

Black, P., and Atkin, M.J. (Eds.). (1996). *Changing the subject: Innovations in science, mathematics and technology education.* London: Routledge.

Briars, D.J., and Resnick, L.B. (2000). *Standards, assessments—and what else? The essential elements of standards-based school improvement.* CSE Technical Report 528. Los Angeles, CA: University of California, Center for the Study of Evaluation, National Center for Research on Evaluation, Standards, and Student Testing.

Bybee, R.W. (1997). *Achieving scientific literacy: From purposes to practices.* Portsmouth, NH: Heinemann.

Carnegie Forum on Education and the Economy. (1986). *A nation prepared: Teachers for the 21st century. The report of the Task Force on Teaching as a Profession.* Washington, DC: The Forum.

Carpenter, T.P., Fennema, E., Peterson, P.L., Chiang, C., and Loef, M. (1989). Using knowledge of children's mathematical thinking in classroom teaching: An experimental study. *American Educational Research Journal, 26*, 499-532.

Clopton, P., McKeown, E., McKeown, M., and Clopton, J. (1998). *Mathematically correct: Algebra I reviews.* Available: http://www.intres.com/mc/algebra.htm. [Accessed September 13, 2001.]

Clotfeler, C.T., and Ladd, H.F. (1996). Recognizing and rewarding success in public schools. In H.F. Ladd (Ed.), *Holding schools accountable: Performance-based reform in education* (pp. 23-63). Washington, DC: Brookings Institution.

Cohen, D.K., and Hill, H.G. (2000). Instructional policy and classroom performance: The mathematics reform in California. *Teachers College Record, 102*(2), 294-343.

Collins, A. (1997). National Science Education Standards: Looking Backward and Forward. *The Elementary School Journal, 97*(4), 299-313.

Conference Board on Mathematical Sciences. (2000). *CBMS Mathematical Education of Teachers Project. Draft report—September 2000.* Available: http://www.maa.org/cbms/metdraft/index.htm. [Accessed December 12, 2000.]

Council of Chief State School Officers. (1997). *Mathematics and science content standards and curriculum frameworks: States progress on development and implementation.* Washington, DC: Author.

Council of Chief State School Officers. (1998). *Standards, graduation, assessment, teacher licensure, time and attendance: A 50-state report, August 1998.* Washington DC: Author.

Council of Chief State School Officers. (1999a). *Data from the Annual Survey of State Student Assessment Programs: Data on 1997-1998 statewide student assessment programs, Volume 1 and 2.* Washington, DC: Author.

Council of Chief State School Officers. (1999b). *State indicators of science and mathematics education: State-by-state trends and new indicators from the 1997-98 school year.* Washington, DC: Author.

Council of Chief State School Officers. (2000). *Using data on enacted curriculum in mathematics and science: Sample results from a study of classroom practices and subject content.* Washington, DC: Author.

Darling-Hammond, L. (2000, January). *Teaching for America's future: A progress report for the millennium, Congressional Program, 15*(1), 53-66. Paper presented at a conference in Aspen, CO.

Davis, A., and Armstrong, J. (1990). State initiatives in assessing science education. In *This Year in School Science 1990: Assessment in the Service of Reform.* Washington, DC: American Association for the Advancement of Science.

DeBoer, G. (1991). *History of ideas in science education.* New York: Teachers College Press.

Dugger, W.E. (2000). Standards for technological literacy. *The Technology Teacher, 59*(5), 8-13.

Dugger, W.E. (2001). Standards for technological literacy. *Phi Delta Kappan, 82*(7), 513-517.

Dwyer, C.A. (1998). Assessment and Classroom Learning: Theory and Practice. *Assessment in Education, 5*(1), 131-137.

Education Commission of the States. (1983). *A 50-state survey of initiatives in science, mathematics and computer education.* ECS Working Papers, No. SM-83-1. Task Force on Education for Economic Growth. Denver, CO: Author.

Education Trust. (1999a). Not Good Enough: A Content Analysis of Teacher Licensing Examinations. *Thinking K-16, 3*(1). Washington, DC: Author.

Education Trust. (1999b). Ticket to Nowhere: The Gap Between Leaving High School and Entering College and High-Performance Jobs. *Thinking K-16, 3*(2). Washington, DC: Author.

Education Week. (2001, January). Special Report: *Quality counts 2001: A better balance: Standards, tests, and the tools to succeed.* Seeking Stability for Standards-Based Education *20*(17).

Fennema, E., Franke, M.L., Carpenter, T.P., and Carey, D. (1993). Using children's mathematical knowledge in instruction. *American Educational Research Journal, 30*, 555-583.

Ferrini-Mundy, J. and Schram, T. (1997). Highlights and Implications. In Ferrini-Mundy, J. and Schram, T. (Eds.) *The Recognizing and Recording Reform in Mathematics Education Project: Insights, Issues, and Implications* in *Journal for Research in Mathematics Education Monograph No.8.* Reston, VA: National Council of Teachers of Mathematics.

Fuhrman, S. and Elmore, R.F. (1994). Governors and education policy in the 1990s. In R.F. Elmore and S. Fuhrman (Eds.), *The Governance of Curriculum. 1994 Yearbook of the Association for Supervision and Curriculum Development.* Alexandria, VA: Association for Supervision and Curriculum Development.

Fullan, M. (2000). The return of large-scale reform. *Journal of Educational Change, 1*, 5-28.

Garet, M. S., Birman, B.F., Porter, A.C., Desimone, L., Herman, R., and Yoon, K.S. (1999). *Designing effective professional development: Lessons from the Eisenhower Program.* Washington, DC: U.S. Department of Education.

Glaser, R., and Silver, E. (1994). Assessment, Testing, and Instruction: Retrospect and Prospect. In L. Darling-Hammond (Ed.), *Review of Research in Education.* Washington, DC: American Educational Research Association.

Goertz, M.E. (2000). Implementing standards-based reform: Challenges for state policy. In T. Duggan and M. Holmes (Eds.), *Closing the gap*, (pp. 65-82). Washington, DC: Council for Basic Education.

Grissmer, D., and Flanagan, A. (1998). *Exploring rapid achievement gains in North Carolina and Texas.* Washington, DC: National Education Goals Panel.

Grossman, P.L., and Stodolsky, S.S. (1995). Content as Context: The Role of School Subjects in Secondary School Teaching. *Educational Researcher, 24*, 5-11.

Haertel, E.H. (1999). Performance Assessment and Education Reform. *Phi Delta Kappan, 80*(9), 662-666.

Hebel, S. (2001, February 9). The Universities Push to Influence State Tests for High-School Students. *The Chronicle of Higher Education.*

Hirsch, E., Koppich, J.E., and Knapp, M.S. (2000). *Revisiting what states are doing to improve the quality of teaching*—A CTP Working Paper. College of Education, University of Washington, Seattle. Available: http://depts.washington.edu/ctpmail/. [Accessed December 12, 2000.]

Humphrey, D.C., Anderson, L., Marsh, J., Marder, C., and Shields, P.M. (1997). *Eisenhower mathematics and science state curriculum frameworks projects: Final evaluation report.* Washington, DC: U.S. Department of Education.

Hurd, P.D. (1960). Science education for changing times. *Rethinking Science Education.* Fifty-ninth Yearbook of the National Society for the Study of Education. Chicago: University of Chicago Press.

Hurd, P.D., and Gallagher, J.J. (1968). *New directions in elementary science education.* San Francisco: Wadsworth.

Ingersoll, R. (1998). The Problem of Out-of-Field Teaching. *Phi Delta Kappan, 79*(10), 773-776.

International Technology Education Association. (1996). *Technology for all Americans: A rationale and structure for the study of technology.* Reston, VA: Author.

International Technology Education Association. (2000). *Standards for technological literacy: Content for the study of technology.* Reston, VA: Author.

Johnson, J., and Aulicino, C. (1998). *Summing it up: A review of survey data on education and the national education goals. A report from Public Agenda.* New York: Public Agenda.

Keller, B. (2000). Elections Seen as Mandate for Bipartisan School Policy. *Education Week, 10*(11), 14 and 19-20.

Kelley, C., Odden, A., Milanowski, A., and Heneman III, H. (2000). The motivational effects of school-based performance awards. CPRE Policy Brief RB-29. Available: http://www.gse.upenn.edu/cpre/frames/pubs.html. [Accessed December 13, 2000.]

Kennedy, M. (1998). *Form and substance in inservice teacher education.* Research Monograph No. 13. Madison, WI: University of Wisconsin, National Institute for Science Education.

Kirst, M.W., Anhalt, B., and Marine, R. (1997). Politics of science education standards. *The Elementary School Journal, 97*(4), 315-328.

Kirst, M.W., and Bird, R.L. (1997). The politics of developing and sustaining mathematics and science curriculum content standards. *Advances in Educational Administration, 5*, 107-132.

Klein, D. (2000). *Testimony of David Klein: April 4, 2000: Before the U.S. House of Representatives Committee on Appropriations' Subcommittee on Labor, Health and Human Services, Education and Related Activities.* Available: http://mathematicallycorrect.com/house.htm. [Accessed June 11, 2001.]

Klein, S., Hamilton, L., McCoffey, D., and Stecher, B. (2000). *What do test scores in Texas tell us?* Available: http://www.rand.org/publications/. [Accessed July 14, 2000.]

Koretz, D. (1998). Large-scale portfolio assessments in the U.S.: Evidence pertaining to the quality of measurement. *Assessment in Education: Principles, Policy & Practice, 5*(2), 309-334.

Koretz, D., Linn, R.L., Dunbar, S.B., and Shepard, L.A. (1991). The effects of high-stakes testing on achievement: Preliminary findings about generalization across tests. Paper presented at the annual meeting of the American Educational Research Association. Chicago, IL: AERA.

Lewis, L., Parsad, B., Carey, N., Bartafi, N., Farris, E., Smerdon, B., and Greene, B. (1999). *Teacher quality: A report on the preparation and qualifications of public school teachers.* Washington, DC: National Center for Education Statistics, U.S. Department of Education.

Linn, R. L. (2000). Assessments and accountability. *Educational Researcher, 29*(2), 4-16.

Linn, R.L., and Herman, J.L. (1997). Standards-Led Assessment: Technical and Policy Issues in Measuring School and Student Progress. CSE Technical Report 426. Los Angeles: Center for Research on Evaluation, Standards, and Student Testing.

Little, J.W. (1993). Teachers' professional development in a climate of educational reform. *Educational Evaluation and Policy Analysis, 15*(2), 129-151.

Loucks-Horsley, S., Hewson, P.W., Love, N., and Stiles, K.E. (1998). *Designing professional development for teachers of science and mathematics.* Thousand Oaks, CA: Corwin Press.

Loucks-Horsley, S., and Matsumoto, C. (1999). Research on professional development for teachers of mathematics and science: The state of the scene. *School Science and Mathematics, 99*(5), 258-271.

Madaus, George F. (1988). The Distortion of Teaching and Testing: High-Stakes Testing and Instruction. *Peabody Journal of Education, 65*(3), 29-46.

Martin, M.O., Mullis, I.V.S., Gonzalez, E.J., O'Connor, K.M., Chrostowski, S.J., Gregory, K.D., Smith, T.A., and Garden, R.A. (2001). *Science benchmarking report: TIMSS 1999 – eighth grade.* Boston: International Association of the Evaluation of Educational Achievement (IEA).

Massell, D., Kirst, M., and Hoppe, M. (1997). *Persistence and Change: Standards Based Reform in Nine States* (CPRE Research Report). Philadelphia: University of Pennsylvania, Center for Policy and Education Research.

McKeon, D., Dianda, M., and McLaren, A. (2001). *Advancing standards: A national call for midcourse corrections and next steps.* Washington, DC: National Education Association.

McLaughlin, M.W. (1987). Learning from Experience: Lessons from Policy Implementation, *Educational Evaluation and Policy Analysis, (9)*2, 171-178.

McLaughlin, M.W. (1991). The Rand Change Agent Study: Ten Years Later, In A.R. Odden (Ed.), *Education Policy Implementation* (pp. 143-155). Albany, NY: State University of New York Press.

McLaughlin, M.W. (1993). What matters most in teachers' workplace context? In J.W. Little and M.W. McLaughlin (Eds.), *Teachers work: Individuals, colleagues, and contexts.* New York: Teachers College Press.

McLeod, D.B., Stake, R.E., Schappelle, B.P., Melissinos, M., and Gierl, M.J. (1996). Setting the standards: NCTM's role in the reform of mathematics education. In S.A. Raizen and E.D. Britton (Eds.), *Bold Ventures, Volume 3: Case Studies of U.S. Innovations in Mathematics Education* (pp.15-130). Dordrecht, Netherlands: Kluwer Academic Publishers.

Meyer, R.H. (1996). Value-added indicators of school performance. In E.A. Hanushek and D.W. Jorgenson (Eds.), NRC's *Improving America's schools: The role of incentives*. Washington, DC: National Academy Press.

Miller, J.A. (1989, October 4). Summit's promise: 'Social compact' for reforms. *Education Week*.

Morse, P.M. and the AIBS Review Team. (2001). *A Review of Biological Instructional Materials for Secondary Schools*. Available: http//www.aibs.org. [Accessed July 5, 2001.] Washington, DC: The American Institute of Biological Sciences.

Mullis, I.V.S., Martin, M.O., Gonzalez, E.J., O'Connor, K.M., Chrostowski, S.J., Gregory, K.D., Garden, R.A. and Smith, T.A. (2001). *Mathematics benchmarking report: TIMSS 1999 – eighth grade*. Boston: International Association of the Evaluation of Educational Achievement (IEA).

National Board for Professional Teaching Standards. (2000a). *Adolescence and young adulthood/mathematics: Standards (for teachers of students ages 14-18+)*. 2nd ed. Arlington, VA: Author.

National Board for Professional Teaching Standards. (2000b). *Early adolescence/ science: standards (for teachers of students ages 11-15)*. Arlington, VA: Author.

National Board for Professional Teaching Standards. (2001). *Assessment and certification*. Available: http//www.nbpts.org. [Accessed September 7, 2001.]

National Center for Education Statistics. (1995). *Teacher supply, teacher qualifications, and teacher turnover, aspects of teacher supply and demand in the U.S., 1990-91*. Washington, DC: U.S. Department of Education.

National Center for Education Statistics. (1996). *Pursuing excellence: A study of United States eighth-grade mathematics and science teaching, learning, curriculum, and achievement in international context*. Washington, DC: U.S. Government Printing Office.

National Center for Education Statistics. (1997a). *Access to postsecondary education for the 1992 high school graduates*, NCES 98-105, by L. Berkner and L. Chavez, MPR Associates, C.D. Carroll, Project officer. Washington DC: U.S. Department of Education.

National Center for Education Statistics. (1997b). *America's teachers: Profile of a profession, 1993-94*. Washington, DC: U.S. Department of Education.

National Center for Education Statistics. (1997c). *Condition of Education 1997*. Washington, DC: U.S. Department of Education.

National Center for Education Statistics. (1999). *Characteristics of the 100 largest public elementary and secondary school districts in the United States: 1997-98*. Washington, DC: U.S. Department of Education.

National Center for Education Statistics. (2000a). *The Condition of education 2000*. Washington, DC: U.S. Department of Education.

National Center for Education Statistics. (2000b). *Digest of education statistics, 1999*. Washington, DC: U.S. Department of Education.

National Center for Education Statistics. (2000c). *Pursuing excellence: Comparisons of international eighth-grade mathematics and science achievement from a U.S. perspective, 1995 and 1999*. Washington, DC: U.S. Department of Education.

National Commission on Excellence in Education. (1983). *A nation at risk: The imperative for educational reform.* Washington, DC: U.S. Department of Education.

National Commission on Mathematics and Science Teaching for the 21st Century. (2000). *Before it's too late: A report to the nation from the National Commission on Mathematics and Science Teaching for the 21st Century.* Washington, DC: U.S. Department of Education.

National Council on Education Standards and Testing. (1992). *Raising standards for American education.* Washington, DC: U.S. Government Printing Office.

National Council of Teachers of Mathematics. (1970). *A History of mathematics education in the United States and Canada.* Washington, DC: Author.

National Council of Teachers of Mathematics. (1989). *Curriculum and evaluation standards for school mathematics.* Reston, VA: Author.

National Council of Teachers of Mathematics. (1991). *Professional standards for teaching mathematics.* Reston, VA: Author.

National Council of Teachers of Mathematics. (1995). *Assessment standards for school mathematics.* Reston, VA: Author.

National Council of Teachers of Mathematics. (2000). *Principles and standards for school mathematics.* Reston, VA: Author.

National Education Goals Panel, (1996). *National education goals report: Building a nation of learners.* Washington, DC: U.S. Government Printing Office.

National Governors Association. (1990). *Educating America: State strategies for achieving the national education goals.* Washington, DC: Author.

National Research Council. (1993). *Measuring up: Prototypes for mathematics assessment.* Washington, DC: National Academy Press.

National Research Council. (1996). *National science education standards.* Washington, DC: National Academy Press.

National Research Council. (1997). *Introducing the national science education standards.* Washington, DC: National Academy Press.

National Research Council. (1999a). *Global perspectives for local action: Using TIMSS to improve local action.* Washington, DC: National Academy Press.

National Research Council. (1999b). *High stakes: Testing for tracking, promotion, and graduation*, J. P. Heubert and R. M. Hauser, (Eds.) Washington, DC: National Academy Press.

National Research Council. (1999c). *How people learn: Brain, mind, experience, and school*, J.D. Bransford, A.L. Brown, and R.R. Cocking, (Eds.) Washington, DC: National Academy Press.

National Research Council. (1999d). *Keeping score*, A. Shannon, (Ed.) Washington, DC: National Academy Press.

National Research Council. (1999e). *Selecting instructional materials: A guide for k-12 science.* M. Singer, and J. Tuomi, (Eds.) Washington DC: National Academy Press.

National Research Council. (1999f). *Testing, teaching, and learning.* Washington, DC: National Academy Press.

National Research Council. (2000). *Educating teachers of science, mathematics, and technology: New practices for the new millennium.* Washington, DC: National Academy Press.

National Research Council. (2001a). *Classroom assessment and the national science education standards.* Washington, DC: National Academy Press.

National Research Council. (2001b). *Testing teacher candidates: The role of licensure tests in improving teacher quality*. K. Mitchell, D. Robinson, B. Plake, and K. Knowles, (Eds.) Washington, DC: National Academy Press.

National Research Council and National Council of Teachers of Mathematics. (1997). *Improving student learning in mathematics and science: The role of national standards in state policy*. G. Burrill and D. Kennedy, Principal Investigators. Washington, DC: National Academy Press.

National Science Foundation. (1996). *Indicators of science and mathematics education 1995*. NSF 96-52, L.E. Suter, (Ed.) Arlington, VA: Author.

National Science Resources Center. (1999). Interview with Nancy Thomas: Investing time as well as dollars. *ScienceLink, 11*(2).

National Science Teachers Association. (1992). *Scope, sequence, and coordination of secondary school science. Volume 1: The content core: A guide for curriculum developers*. Washington, DC: Author.

National Science Teachers Association. (1998). NSTA position statement: NSTA standards for science teacher preparation. Available: http://199.0.3.5/handbook/prep.asp. [Accessed December 12, 2000.]

Niyogi, N.S. (1995). *The intersection of instruction and assessment: The classroom*. Princeton, NJ: Educational Testing Service Policy Information Center.

North Carolina Public Schools. (2000). North Carolina National Board for Professional Teaching Standards. Available: http://www.ncpublicschools.org/nbpts/. [Accessed January 26, 2001.]

Oakes, J., Ormseth, T.H., Bell, R.M., and Camp, P. (1990). *Multiplying inequalities: The effects of race, social class, and tracking on opportunities to learn mathematics and science*. Santa Monica, CA: RAND.

O'Day, J.A., and Smith, M.S. (1993). Systemic Reform and Educational Opportunity. In S.H. Fuhrman, (Ed.), *Designing Coherent Education Policy: Improving the System* (pp. 313-322). San Francisco: Jossey-Bass.

Olson, L. (2001). Finding the Right Mix. In *Education Week* Special report: *Quality Counts 2001: A Better Balance: Standards, Tests, and the Tools to Succeed.* Seeking Stability for Standards-Based Education. *20*(17), 12-20.

Popham, W.J. (2000). *Modern educational measurement: Practical guidelines for educational leaders*. Needham, MA: Allyn & Bacon.

Public Agenda. (2000). *Survey finds little sign of backlash against academic standards or standardized tests*. New York: Author.

Raizen, S.A. (1991). The reform of science education in the U.S.A. déjà vu or de novo? *Studies in Science Education, 19*, 1-41.

Raizen, S.A. (1998). Standards for Science Education. *Teachers College Record 100*(1), 66-121.

Ravitch, D. (1995). *National standards in American education: A citizen's guide.* Washington, DC: Brookings Institute.

Resnick, L., and Resnick, D. (1992). Assessing the thinking curriculum: New tools for educational reform. In B. Gifford and M. O'Connor (Eds.), *Changing Assessment: Alternative Views of Aptitude, Achievement, and Instruction*, pp. 37-76. Norwell, MA: Kluwer Academic Publishers.

Riley, R.W. (2000). Seventh annual state of American education address: Setting new expectations. Southern High School, Durham, North Carolina, February 22, 2000. Available: http://www.ed.gov/Speeches/02-2000/000222.html. [Accessed January 8, 2001.]

Robelen, E. (2000, July 31). Education takes center stage at GOP convention. *Education Week, 19*(43).

Robitaille, D., Schmidt, W., Raizen, S., McKnight, C., Britton, E., and Nicol, C. (1993). *Curriculum frameworks for mathematics and science.* (Third International Mathematics and Science Study: Monograph No. 1). Vancouver, Canada: Pacific Educational Press.

Romberg, T. (1998). Comments: NCTM's Curriculum and Evaluation Standards. *Teachers College Record, 100*(1), 8-21.

Rose, L.C., and Gallup, A.M. (2000). *The 32nd annual Phi Delta Kappa/Gallup Poll of the public's attitudes toward the public schools.* Bloomington, IN: Phi Delta Kappa International, Inc.

Rothman, F.G., and Narum, J.L. (2000). *Then, now, and in the next decade: A commentary on strengthening undergraduate science, mathematics, and engineering education.* Washington, DC: Project Kaleidoscope.

Sack, J.L., and Jacobson, L. (2000, August 18). Gore calls education "number-one priority." *Education Week, 19*(43).

Shepard, L.A. (1991). Negative policies for dealing with diversity: When does assessment and diagnosis turn into sorting and segregation? In E.H. Hiebert, (Ed.), *Literacy for a diverse society: Perspectives, practices, and policies* (pp. 279-298). New York: Teachers College Press.

Shepard, L.A. (2000). *The role of classroom assessment in teaching and learning.* CRESST CSE Technical Report. National Center for Research on Evaluation, Standards, and Student Testing (CRESST) Center for the Study of Evaluation Center for Research on Education, Diversity and Excellence. Los Angeles: University of California.

Shields, P.M., Esch, C.E., Humphrey, D.C., Young, V.M., Gaston, M., and Hunt, H. (1999). *The status of the teaching profession: Research findings and policy recommendations. A report to the teaching and California's future task force.* Santa Cruz, CA: The Center for the Future of Teaching and Learning.

Shulman, L. (1986). Those who understand: Knowledge growth in teaching. *Educational Researcher, 15*(2), 4-14.

Shulman, L. (1987). Knowledge and teaching: Foundations of the new reform. *Harvard Educational Review,* 57, 1-22.

Smith, M.S., and O'Day, J.A. (1991). Systemic School Reform. In S. Fuhrman and B. Malen, (Eds.), *Politics of Curriculum and Testing: The 1990 Yearbook of the Politics of Education Association* (pp. 233-267). London: Falmer.

Spillane, J.P., and Callahan, K.A. (2000). Implementing state standards for science education: What district policymakers make of the hoopla. *Journal of Research in Science Teaching, 37*(5), 401-425.

Stake, R., and Easley, J. (1978). *Case studies in science education.* Urbana, IL: University of Illinois at Urbana-Champaign, Center for Instructional Research and Curriculum Evaluation.

Stecher, B. (1998). The local benefits and burdens of large-scale portfolio assessments. *Assessment in Education: Principles, Policy & Practice, 5*(2), 335-351.

Stecher, B.M., Barron, S., Kaganoff, T., and Goodwin, J. (1998). *The effects of standards-based assessment on classroom practices: Results of the 1996-97 RAND survey of Kentucky teachers of mathematics and writing.* CSE Technical Report 482. Los Angeles: Center for Research on Evaluation, Standards, and Student Testing.

Stecher, B.M. and Barron, S.I. (1999). *Quadrennial milepost accountability testing in Kentucky*. CSE Technical Report. National Center for Research on Evaluation, Standards, and Student Testing (CRESST) Center for the Study of Evaluation (CSE)/ RAND. Los Angeles: University of California.

Stigler J.W., and Hiebert, J. (1999). *The teaching gap: Best ideas from the world's teachers for improving education in the classroom*. New York: Free Press.

Stricherz, M. (2001, March). Governors Seeking Levers to Improve Education. *Education Week, 20*(28), 1-17.

Talbert, J.E., and McLaughlin, M.W. (1993). Understanding teaching in context. In D.K. Cohen, M.W. McLaughlin, and J.E. Talbert, (Eds.), *Teaching for Understanding: Challenges for Policy and Practice* (pp. 167-206). San Francisco: Jossey-Bass.

Thompson, C.L., Spillane, J., and Cohen, D.K. (1994). *The state policy system affecting science and mathematics education in Michigan*. East Lansing, MI: MSSI Policy and Program Review Component, Michigan Partnership for New Education.

Tyack, D., and Cuban, L. (1995). *Tinkering toward Utopia: A century of public school reform*. Cambridge, MA: Harvard University Press.

Tyson, H. (1997). *Overcoming Structural Barriers to Good Textbooks*. Available: http://www.negp.gov/reports/tyson.htm. [Accessed February 8, 2001.]

U.S. Department of Education. (1991). *America 2000: An education strategy*. Washington, DC: U.S. Government Printing Office.

U.S. Department of Education. (1999). *Promising results, continuing challenges: The final report of the national assessment of Title I*. Washington, DC: U.S. Government Printing Office.

U.S. Department of Education. (2000a). *The federal role in education*. Washington, DC: Author.

U.S. Department of Education. (2000b). *U.S. Department of Education's 1999 performance report and 2001 annual plan. Volume 1: Department-wide objectives*. Washington, DC: Author.

U.S. Department of Education's Mathematics and Science Expert Panel. (2000). *Exemplary and promising mathematics programs 1999*. Washington, DC: U.S. Department of Education.

Walsh, M. (2000, November 8). Harcourt General, Inc. agrees to terms of sale. *Education Week, 20*(10), 13.

Weiss, I.R. (1978). *Report of the 1977 national survey of science, mathematics, and social studies education*. Research Triangle Park, NC: Research Triangle Institute.

Weiss, I.R. (1987). *Report of the 1985-86 national survey of science and mathematics education*. Research Triangle Park, NC: Research Triangle Institute.

Weiss, I.R. (1991). *Curricular materials for mathematics and science: Usage and perceived needs from the field*. Chapel Hill, NC: Horizon Research, Inc.

Weiss, I.R., Matti, M.C., and Smith, P.S. (1994). *Report of the 1993 national survey of science and mathematics education*. Chapel Hill, NC: Horizon Research, Inc.

White, P.A., Porter, A.C., Gamoran, A., and Smithson, J. (1996). *Upgrading high school math: A look at three transition courses*. CPRE Policy Briefs. Philadelphia: University of Pennsylvania, CPRE. Available: http://www.upenn.edu/gse/cpre. [Accessed September 4, 2001.]

Wilson, S.M., and Berne, J. (1999). Teacher learning and the acquisition of professional knowledge: An examination of research on contemporary professional development. *Review of Research in Education, 24*, 173-209.

Woodward, A., and Elliott, D.L. (1990). Textbooks: Consensus and Controversy. In *Textbooks and Schooling in the United States: Eighty-ninth Yearbook of the National Society for the Study of Education*, Part I. Chicago: University of Chicago Press.

Wulf, W.A. (2000). The standards for technological literacy: A National Academies perspective. *The Technology Teacher, 59*(6), 10-12.

PARTICIPANTS AT THE WORKSHOP ON UNDERSTANDING THE INFLUENCE OF STANDARDS IN K-12 SCIENCE, MATHEMATICS, AND TECHNOLOGY EDUCATION

MAY 31–JUNE 1, 2000
WASHINGTON, D.C.

Invited Participants

Mitchell D. Chester
Executive Director for Accountability and Assessment
School District of Philadelphia
2120 Winter Street, Room 406
Philadelphia, PA 19103

Jere Confrey
Professor
Department of Curriculum and Instruction
University of Texas at Austin
1912 Speedway, SZB 105700, 78705
Austin, TX 78712

Anthony Gilberti
Professor
Industrial Technology Education Department
School of Technology
Indiana State University
219B Technology Center
Terre Haute, IN 47809

David Grissmer
Associate Research Director
RAND
1200 S. Hayes Street
Arlington, VA 22202

Maryellen Harmon
Science and Mathematics Consultant
135 Maplewood Street
Watertown, MA 02472-1408

Michael Lang
Director of Science Programs
Maricopa Community Colleges District
2411 West 14th Street
Tempe, AZ 85281-6942

Carolyn R. Mahoney
Founding Faculty
Department Chair and Professor of Mathematics
Department of Mathematics
California State University, San Marcos
San Marcos, CA 92096-0001

Shirley Malcom
Director
Directorate for Education and Human Resources
American Association for the Advancement of Science
1200 New York Avenue, NW
Washington, DC 20005

Judith Mumme
Co-Principal Investigator
Videocases for Mathematics Professional Development and Mathematics Renaissance K-12
VCSSO
570 Airport Way
Camarillo, CA 93010-8500

Greg Pearson
Program Officer
National Academy of Engineering
2101 Constitution Avenue, NW
Washington, DC 20418

Senta A. Raizen
Director
National Center for Improving Science Education/WestEd
1726 M Street, NW, Suite 704
Washington DC 20036

Carolyn Ray
Director
Urban Systemic Initiative
Cleveland Municipal School District
1380 East 6th Street, R
Room 227
Cleveland, OH 44114

Judy Roitman
Mathematics Professor
University of Kansas
Lawrence, KS 66045

Ethel Schulz
Science Education Consultant
158 Whalers Lane
Salem, MA 01970

Deborah C. Smith
Assistant Professor
Science Education
324 Erickson Hall
Michigan State University
East Lansing, MI 48824

William Trent
Professor
Educational Policy Studies and Sociology
University of Illinois
College of Education, Room 368
Champaign, IL 61820

Rachel E. Wood
Education Associate
Delaware Department of Education
Science Resource Center
655 Glenwood Avenue
Smyrna, DE 19977-1206

Sponsor Representatives

Janice M. Earle
Program Director
Division of Elementary, Secondary, and Informal Education
National Science Foundation
4201 Wilson Boulevard
Arlington, VA 22230

Jane Butler Kahle
Division Director
Division of Elementary, Secondary, and Informal Education
National Science Foundation
4201 Wilson Boulevard
Arlington, VA 22230

Members, Committee on Understanding the Influence of Standards

Iris R. Weiss, Chair
President
Horizon Research, Inc.
111 Cloister Court
Suite 220
Chapel Hill, NC 27514

Maria Alicia Lopez Freeman
Executive Director
California Science Project
3806 Geology Building
University of California
Los Angeles, CA 90095-1567

Margaret Goertz
Co-Director for the Policy & Governance Program Area
Consortium for Policy Research in Education
Graduate School of Education
University of Pennsylvania
3440 Market Street, Suite 560
Philadelphia, PA 19104-3325

Michael S. Knapp
Director, Center for the Study of Teaching and Policy
University of Washington
College of Education
Miller Hall, M201
Box 353600
Seattle, WA 98195

Mari Muri
Mathematics Consultant
Connecticut Department of Education
P.O. Box 2219
165 Capitol Avenue
Hartford, CT 06145

Patrick Shields
Program Manager
SRI International
333 Ravenswood
Menlo Park, CA 94025

Judith Sowder
Professor
San Diego State University
Department of Mathematical and Computer Science
San Diego, CA 92182-7720

Elizabeth K. Stage
Mathematics Professional Development Initiatives
University of California
Office of the President
300 Lakeside Drive, 7th floor
Oakland, CA 94612

Kendall Starkweather
Executive Director
International Technology Education Association
1914 Association Drive
Reston, VA 20191

P. Uri Treisman
Director
The Charles A. Dana Center for Mathematics and Science Education
University of Texas at Austin
2901 North IH 35, Suite 3.200
Austin, TX 78712

Members, Center for Education's Strategic Planning Advisory Group

Melvin D. George, Chair
President Emeritus and Professor of Mathematics Emeritus
University of Missouri
1509 W. Rollins Road
Columbia, MO 65203

J. Myron Atkin
Professor
Stanford University
School of Education
520 Galvez Mall
Stanford, CA 94305-3096

Joan Ferrini-Mundy
Associate Dean, College of Natural Science
Division of Science and Mathematics Education
Michigan State University
210 North Kedzie Laboratory
East Lansing, MI 48824-1031

Staff, Center for Education

Mailing address:

Center for Education
National Research Council
2101 Constitution Avenue, NW
Harris Building, Room 450
Washington, DC 20418
Fax: 202-334-1453

Gail Burrill
Senior Program Officer
Phone: 202-334-2085
Email: gburrill@nas.edu

Michael Feuer
Executive Director
Phone: 202-334-1868
Email: mfeuer@nas.edu

Karen Hollweg
Senior Program Officer
Phone: 202-334-3055
Email: khollweg@nas.edu

Tina Winters
Senior Project Assistant
Phone: 202-334-3084
Email: twinters@nas.edu

A FRAMEWORK FOR INVESTIGATING THE INFLUENCE OF NATIONALLY DEVELOPED STANDARDS FOR MATHEMATICS, SCIENCE, AND TECHNOLOGY EDUCATION

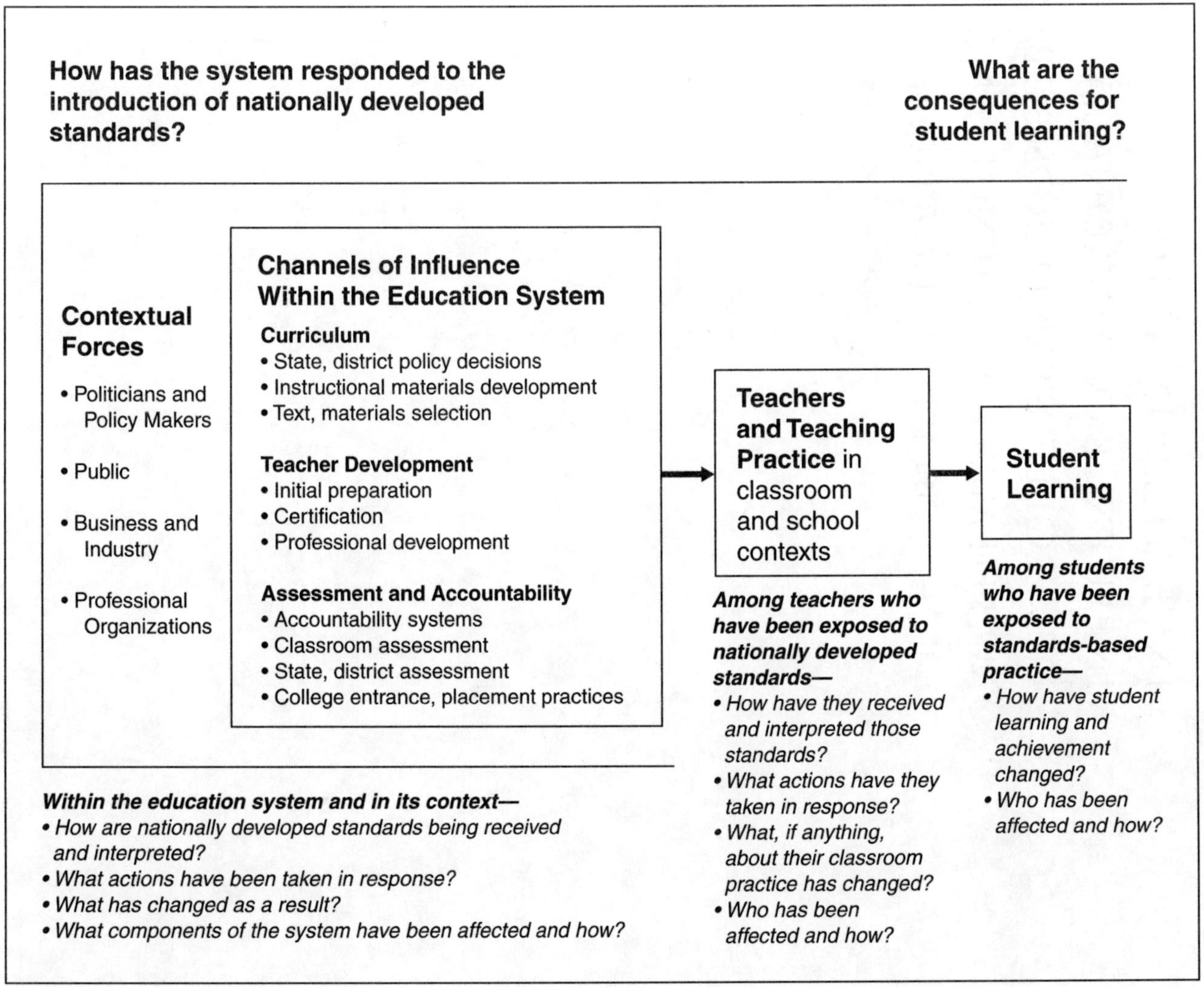

How has the system responded to the introduction of nationally developed standards?
What are the consequences for student learning?
Contextual Forces
• Politicians and Policy Makers
• Public
• Business and Industry
• Professional Organizations
Channels of Influence Within the Education System
Curriculum
• State, district policy decisions
• Instructional materials development
• Text, materials selection
Teacher Development
• Initial preparation
• Certification
• Professional development
Assessment and Accountability
• Accountability systems
• Classroom assessment
• State, district assessment
• College entrance, placement practices
Teachers and Teaching Practice in classroom and school contexts
Student Learning
Within the education system and in its context—
• How are nationally developed standards being received and interpreted?
• What actions have been taken in response?
• What has changed as a result?
• What components of the system have been affected and how?
Among teachers who have been exposed to nationally developed standards—
• How have they received and interpreted those standards?
• What actions have they taken in response?
• What, if anything, about their classroom practice has changed?
• Who has been affected and how?
Among students who have been exposed to standards-based practice—
• How have student learning and achievement changed?
• Who has been affected and how?

BIOGRAPHICAL SKETCHES

Iris R. Weiss (Chair) is president of Horizon Research, Inc. (HRI) in Chapel Hill, North Carolina. Prior to establishing HRI in 1987, Dr. Weiss was senior research scientist at the Research Triangle Institute. Her activities have included directing national surveys of science and mathematics teachers; evaluating science and mathematics education projects and systemic reform efforts; and providing technical assistance to agencies and professional organizations such as the U.S. Department of Education, American Association for the Advancement of Science, Council of Chief State School Officers, National Council of Teachers of Mathematics, National Science Teachers Association, and Office of Technology Assessment. She is currently directing the design and implementation of an 80-project cross-site evaluation of National Science Foundation's Local Systemic Change Initiative; the development of a database of materials for the professional development of mathematics and science teachers; and an observational study of a sample of more than 400 mathematics and science classes throughout the United States. Dr. Weiss has a B.S. in biology from Cornell University, a master's in science education from Harvard University, and a Ph.D. in curriculum and instruction from the University of North Carolina at Chapel Hill.

William Browder is a professor of mathematics at Princeton University and a member of the National Academy of Sciences. After teaching at the University of Rochester and Cornell University, he joined the Princeton Mathematics Department in 1963, and served as chairman from1971-73. He served as an editor of the *Annals of Mathematics* from 1969-81. Among the many visiting positions he has held are appointments at the universities of Oxford, Paris, Chicago, Northwestern, Aarhus, as well as the Institute for Advanced Study and the Max Planck Institute in Bonn. He was chairman of the Office of Math Sciences of the National Research Council from 1978-84. In this position, he organized the David Committee Study on the health of the mathematical sciences, as well as serving as chairman of the briefing panel for mathematics for the White House Office of Science and Technology Policy. Dr. Browder has been elected to many offices in the American Mathematical Society including a member of the Council and vice president, and served as president from 1989-91. Dr. Browder received his undergraduate degree from MIT, and a Ph.D. from Princeton.

Gail Burrill is a senior program officer and director of the Mathematical Sciences Education Board at the National Research Council. She was a secondary teacher and department chair in suburban Milwaukee, Wisconsin, for over 25 years and spent time as an associate researcher at the University of Wisconsin–Madison. She is a past president of the National Council of Teachers of Mathematics. As an instructor for Teachers Teaching with Technology, she conducts workshops around the country on using technology in the classroom. Her honors include the Presidential Award for Excellence in Teaching Mathematics and the Wisconsin Distinguished Educator Award. She was elected a fellow of the American Statistical Association and was awarded an honorary doctorate degree from Rose-Hulman Institute of Technology. She was on the National Board for Professional Teaching Standards, is currently a member of the Advisory Board of the Woodrow Wilson National Fellowship Foundation, and a director of the senior high school component of the Park City Mathematics Institute. The author of numerous books and articles on statistics and mathematics education, she has spoken nationally and internationally on issues in mathematics education. She has an undergraduate degree in mathematics from Marquette University and a master's in mathematics from Loyola University of Chicago.

Maria Alicia Lopez Freeman is the executive director of the California Science Project and the director for the Center for Teacher Leadership in Language and Status Issues. She has taught chemistry and physics in large urban inner-city high schools and served as department chairperson. For the past 10 years, she has been working in science professional development, science education research, and educational change. She is currently involved in science education research primarily through the development of case studies focused on teachers and students of color in science programs. She served on the National Commission on Mathematics and Science Teaching for the 21st Century. She was twice elected the chairperson of the California Curriculum Development and Supplemental Materials Commission, an advisory body to the California State Board of Education. She was actively involved with the development of the National Science Education Standards as a member of the Working Group on Science Teaching Standards. She served as a member of the committee on Adolescence and Young Adulthood Science Standards for the National Board for Professional Teaching Standards. She was appointed to the Expert Panel in Mathematics and Science Education for the U.S. Department of Education and served on the board of directors of BSCS. Ms. Lopez Freeman has a degree in chemistry and physics and a master's degree in educational leadership and change from Immaculate Heart College.

Michael Fullan is the dean of the Ontario Institute for Studies in Education of the University of Toronto. He has developed a number of partnerships designed to bring about major school improvement and educational reform. He participates as researcher, consultant, trainer, and policy advisor on a range of educational change projects with school systems, teachers' federations, research and development institutes, and government agencies in Canada and internationally. Dr. Fullan is currently leading the evaluation team conducting a four-year assessment of England's National Literacy and Numeracy Strategy. His most recent books are *The New Meaning of Educational Change* (3rd Edition) and *Leading in a Culture of Change.* He has a Ph.D. in sociology from the University of Toronto.

Margaret Goertz is a professor of education policy and a co-director of the Consortium for Policy Research in Education (CPRE) at the Graduate School of Education, University of Pennsylvania, where she directs the CPRE research program in education policy and governance. Over the past 20 years, she has studied education finance systems, with particular attention to education policy and intergovernmental relations, and to fiscal and programmatic equity and students with special needs. Her current research focuses on how states, school districts, schools, and teachers implement federal and state standards, assessment, and accountability policies. Dr. Goertz recently completed a study for the U.S. Department of Education of accountability policies in all 50 states and their interface with Title I policies, and a more in-depth study of how teachers, schools, and school districts implement state standards, assessment, and accountability policies in eight states and 23 school districts. She has published five books and more than three dozen chapters, articles, and monographs on education policy and education finance. Dr. Goertz has a Ph.D. in social science from the Maxwell School of Syracuse University.

Karen S. Hollweg is senior program officer and directs the Committee on Science Education K-12 at the National Research Council. Prior to joining the NRC, she worked as a public school science teacher and district administrator and directed community-based education projects. As the principal investigator of many National Science Foundation grants, she has led the design, implementation, and dissemination of informal science education, teacher enhancement, and curriculum development projects. Ms. Hollweg has authored many books and articles about urban ecosystem education, scientist-teacher collaborations, and team-based professional development. She has served on advisory committees and boards of many national education projects and organizations, and has been a consultant on environmental education projects internationally. Ms. Hollweg has a B.A. in biology and a M.A. in science education from Stanford University.

Michael S. Knapp is currently professor and chair, Educational Leadership and Policy Studies, at the University of Washington, and also director of the Center for the Study of Teaching and Policy, a national Research and Development Center supported by the U.S. Department of Education. Dr. Knapp's teaching and research focuses on educational policy-making and policy implementation, the connections between policy and classroom practice or school improvement, and the ways education serves various populations, especially disenfranchised groups. Dr. Knapp's research pays special attention to the influence of leadership and policy environments on the quality of teaching, the teacher workforce, and the development of teachers' capacities. In both his working experience as a junior high school science teacher and as a policy researcher, Dr. Knapp's work has often focused on mathematics and science education, and how it can be improved. Dr. Knapp has written extensively about his research, including several recent books, *Teaching for Meaning in High-Poverty Classrooms* and *Paths to Partnership: University and Community as Learners in Interprofessional Education.* Dr. Knapp received a Ph.D. in sociology of education from Stanford University.

Paul LeMahieu is Hawaii's State Superintendent. In the past, Dr. LeMahieu served as principal investigator for the Delaware Statewide Systemic Initiative for the reform of mathematics and science education, and served for 11 years as director of research, evaluation, and student assessment for the Pittsburgh (Pennsylvania) Board of Public Education. He has received major awards for his contributions to educational theory and practice from the American Educational Research Association, Evaluation Research Society, Buros Institute of Measurement, National Association of Test Directors, and Association for Supervision and Curriculum Development. Dr. LeMahieu has served as president of the National Association of Test Directors and vice president of the American Educational Research Association. He has degrees from Yale College (A.B., 1974), Harvard University (Ed.M., 1977), and the University of Pittsburgh (Ph.D.,1983).

Mari Muri is a mathematics consultant for the Connecticut State Department of Education. Ms. Muri has been a co-principal investigator for Connecticut's National Science Foundation State Systemic Initiative Award, the co-author of *Mathematics Activities for Elementary School Teachers: A Problem Solving Approach*, 4th Edition, and a member of the National Council of Teachers of Mathematics writing team of *Assessment Standards for School Mathematics*, 1995. She has taught at the elementary school level and since 1985 at the postsecondary school level. Her awards include the Robert A. Rosenbaum Award for Excellence in Serving the Connecticut Mathematics Community from the Association of Teachers of Mathematics in Connecticut; Connecticut 1994 Educational Leader of the Year; and Who's Who in American Education, 1993. She was a member of the Association of State Supervisors of Mathematics Executive Board from 1995-99, and its president from 1996-98. She has also been on the executive board of the Association of Teachers of Mathematics in Connecticut from 1988 to the present. Ms. Muri is a member of the National Educational Honor Societies and the

Mathematical Sciences Education Board. She has been active in professional workshops, activities, presentations, and community service. She has a master's degree in education from Eastern Connecticut State University and a Sixth-year Certificate in Educational Leadership from the University of Connecticut.

Patrick M. Shields is director of the Center on Education Policy at SRI International. Dr. Shields is also currently director of research for Teaching and California's Future, an examination of the status of the teaching workforce in the state and is co-director of the evaluation of the Pew Network for Standards-Based Reform. In these positions, he has had the opportunity to examine issues surrounding standards, teacher professional development, and assessment. Dr. Shields' career has been devoted to research on efforts to improve schooling, especially for students at risk of failure. His most recent publications include *When Theory Hits Reality: Standards-Based Reform in Urban Districts* and *The Status of the Teaching Profession 2000*. Dr. Shields serves on the National Council of Mathematics Standards Impact Research Group. He holds a Ph.D. in educational policy from Stanford University.

Judith Sowder is professor emerita of mathematical sciences at San Diego State University. She taught mathematics to elementary, middle, secondary, and college classes before earning a doctorate in 1976. Since then, she has focused on preparing teachers and graduate students in mathematics education and on research on learning and teaching mathematics. Dr. Sowder has received awards for teaching and research, most recently a Lifetime Achievement Award from the National Council of Teachers of Mathematics. She has published over 40 papers in journals and proceedings, 20 book chapters, and four books, all on topics of mathematics learning and teaching. Dr. Sowder is the past editor of the *Journal for Research in Mathematics Education*, is currently co-principal investigator on an IERI grant on integrating mathematics and pedagogy, and is co-director of a newly established professional development collaborative. She has served on many national and international committees and advisory boards. Most recently, she served on the writing team of the new Conference Board of Mathematical Sciences book on the preparation of mathematics teachers, and now serves on the board of directors for the National Council of Teachers of Mathematics. Dr. Sowder has directed numerous projects funded by the National Science Foundation and the U.S. Department of Education. She received her doctorate from the University of Oregon.

Elizabeth K. Stage is director of mathematics and science professional development, educational outreach in the University of California Office of the President, responsible for grants to higher education campuses throughout the state. She has been a local and statewide director for some of these programs; has worked on state and national standards and assessments in mathematics and science; conducted research, program evaluation, and curriculum development at the Lawrence Hall of Science, University of California, Berkeley; and has taught at the elementary and middle school levels and at the graduate level at Berkeley and Harvard. Throughout these activities, she has been guided by a vision of high quality mathematics and science education for all students. She has an Ed.D. in science education from Harvard University.

Kendall Starkweather is executive director of the International Technology Education Association (ITEA). As executive director, Dr. Starkweather is involved in activities designed to advance ITEA's mission of promoting technological literacy in U.S. K-12 schools. He currently oversees the development of standards for technology education in ITEA's Technology for All Americans project and is publisher of the association's two journals, *The Technology Teacher* and *Technology and Children*. He has served as a member of the Board on Engineering Education at the National Research Council. His background includes high school teaching experience and nearly a decade of college-level preservice teacher education work. His efforts have been directed toward development of educational materials on problem-solving and technology and the impacts of technology on people and the environment. He holds a Ph.D. from the University of Maryland.

P. Uri Treisman is professor of mathematics and director of the Charles A. Dana Center at The University of Texas at Austin. He serves as executive director of the National Science Foundation-funded Texas Statewide Systemic Initiative and is president of the board of the Consortium for Mathematics and Its Applications. For his research at the University of California at Berkeley on the factors that support high achievement among minority students in calculus, he received the 1987 Charles A. Dana Award for Pioneering Achievement in American Higher Education. In 1992, he was named a MacArthur Fellow and in December 1999, he was named as one of the outstanding leaders in higher education in the 20th century by the magazine *Black Issues in Higher Education*. Dr. Treisman serves on many national committees, boards, and commissions concerned with mathematics education. He has served on the National Research Council's Coordinating Council for Mathematics, Science and Engineering Education and currently serves on the Committee on a Strategic Education Research Plan for the United States. He is an advisor to national groups including the Department of Defense's Secondary Education Transition Study, which examines the consequences of high mobility among high-school-aged students in military families. He received his Ph.D. at the University of California at Berkeley in 1985.

Marc Tucker is president of the National Center on Education and the Economy, a nonprofit organization based in Washington, DC. Mr. Tucker serves as co-director of New Standards, a national program to create internationally benchmarked academic standards and matching performance examinations for the schools. He served as staff director of the group that created the National Board for Professional Teaching Standards and as the Board's first president. Mr. Tucker is co-author of *Thinking for a Living: Education and the Wealth of Nations* and of *Standards for Our Schools: How to Set Them, Measure Them, and Reach Them*. Mr. Tucker chairs the standards, assessment, and certification policy committee of the National Skill Standards Board. Prior to forming the National Center on Education and the Economy, Mr. Tucker served as associate director of the National Institute of Education, where he directed the Institute's policy research program. Mr. Tucker holds an A.B. degree from Brown University.

INDEX

D

E

F

G

H

I

K

L

M

N

P

Q

S